THE GARDEN OF KAMA

AND OTHER LOVE LYRICS FROM INDIA
Arranged in Verse by LAURENCE HOPE
Illustrated by BYAM SHAW

PUBLISHED BY ROBERT FREDERICK LTD.

Downwood, Claverton Down Road, Bath BA2 6DT

Arranged in verse by Laurence Hope
Illustrations by Byam Shaw

Reproduction in the UK
Printed by BPC Paulton Books Ltd., Paulton, UK

CONTENTS

Contents

Contents

LESS THAN THE DUST

LESS THAN THE DUST, BENEATH THY
Chariot wheel,
Less than the rust, that never stained thy Sword,
Less than the trust thou hast in me,
Oh, Lord, Even less than these !

Less than the weed, that grows beside thy door,
Less than the speed, of hours, spent far from thee,
Less than the need thou hast in life of me.
Even less am I.

Since I, Oh, Lord, am nothing unto thee,
See here thy Sword, I make it keen and bright,
Love's last reward, Death, comes to me to-night,
Farewell, Zahir-u-din.

TO THE UNATTAINABLE

OH, THAT MY BLOOD WERE WATER,
thou athirst,
And thou and I in some far Desert land,
How would I shed it gladly, if but first
It touched thy lips, before it reached the sand.

Once,—Ah, the Gods were good to me,—I threw
Myself upon a poison snake, that crept
Where my Beloved—a lesser love we knew
Than this which now consumes me wholly—slept.

But thou; Alas, what can I do for thee ?
By Fate, and thine own beauty, set above
The need of all or any aid from me,
Too high for service, as too far for love.

IN THE EARLY, PEARLY MORNING: SONG BY VALGOVIND

THE FIELDS ARE FULL OF POPPIES,
and the skies are very blue,
By the Temple in the coppice,
I wait, Beloved, for you.
The level land is sunny,
and the errant air is gay,
With scent of rose & honey;
will you come to me to-day ?

From carven walls above me,
smile lovers; many a pair.
" Oh, take this rose & love me ! "
she has twined it in her hair.
He advances, she retreating,
pursues and holds her fast,
The sculptor left them meeting,
in a close embrace at last.

Through centuries together,
in the carven stone they lie,
In the glow of golden weather,
and endless azure sky.
Oh, that we, who have for pleasure
so short & scant a stay,
Should waste our summer leisure;
will you come to me to-day ?

In the Early, Pearly Morning: Song by Valgovind

The Temple bells are ringing,
  for the marriage month has come.
I hear the women singing,
  and the throbbing of the drum.
And when the song is failing,
  or the drums a moment mute,
The weirdly wistful wailing
  of the melancholy flute.

Little Life has got to offer,
  and little man to lose,
Since to-day Fate deigns to proffer,
  Oh, wherefore, then refuse
To take this transient hour,
  in the dusky Temple gloom
While the poppies are in flower,
  and the mangoe trees abloom.

And if Fate remember later,
  and come to claim her due,
What sorrow will be greater
  than the Joy I had with you ?
For to-day, lit by your laughter,
  between the crushing years,
I will chance, in the hereafter,
  eternities of tears.

REVERIE OF MAHOMED AKRAM AT THE TAMARIND TANK

THE DESERT IS PARCHED
in the burning sun
And the grass is scorched and white.
But the sand is passed,
and the march is done,
We are camping here to-night.
I sit in the shade of the Temple walls,
While the cadenced water evenly falls,
And a peacock out of the Jungle calls
To another, on yonder tomb.
Above, half seen, in the lofty gloom,
Strange works of a long dead people loom,
Obscene and savage and half effaced—
An elephant hunt, a musicians' feast—

And curious matings
of man and beast;
What did they mean to the men
who are long since dust ?
Whose fingers traced,
In this arid waste,
These rioting, twisted, figures of love and lust.

Strange, weird things that no man may say,
Things Humanity hides away;—
Secretly done,—
Catch the light of the living day,
Smile in the sun.

Reverie of Mahomed Akram

Cruel things that man may not name,
Naked here, without fear or shame,
Laugh in the carven stone.

Deep in the Temple's innermost
        Shrine is set,
Where the bats and the shadows dwell,
The worn and ancient
        Symbol of Life, at rest
In its oval shell,
By which the men, who, of old,
        the land possessed,
Represented their Great Destroying Power.
I cannot forget
That, just as my life was
        touching its fullest flower,
Love came and destroyed it
        all in a single hour,
Therefore the dual Mystery suits me well.

Sitting alone,
The tank's deep water is cool and sweet,
Soothing and fresh to the wayworn feet,
Dreaming, under the Tamarind shade,
One silently thanks the men who made
So green a place in this bitter land
Of sunburnt sand.

The Peacocks scream
        and the grey Doves coo,
Little green, talkative Parrots woo,

And small grey squirrels, with fear askance,
At alien me, in their furtive glance,
Come shyly, with quivering fur, to see
The stranger under their Tamarind-tree.

Daylight dies,
The Camp fires redden like angry eyes,
The Tents show white,
In the glimmering light,
Spirals of tremulous smoke arise, to the purple skies,
And the hum of the Camp sounds like the sea,
Drifting over the sand to me.
Afar, in the Desert some wild voice sings
To a jangling zither with minor strings,
And, under the stars growing keen above,
I think of the thing that I love.

A beautiful thing, alert, serene,
With passionate, dreaming, wistful eyes,
Dark and deep as mysterious skies,
Seen from a vessel at sea.
Alas, you drifted away from me,
And Time and Space have rushed in between,
But they cannot undo the Thing-that-has-been,
Though it never again may be.
You were mine, from dusk until dawning light,
For the perfect whole of the bygone night
You belonged to me !

Reverie of Mahomed Akram

They say that Love is a light thing
A foolish thing and a slight thing
A ripe fruit, rotten at core,
They speak in this futile fashion
To me, who am wracked with passion,
Tormented beyond compassion,
For ever and ever more.

They say that Possession lessens a lover's delight,
As radiant mornings fade into afternoon.
I held what I loved in my arms for many a night,
Yet ever the morning lightened the sky too soon.

Beyond our tents the sands stretch level and far,
Around this little oasis of Tamarind trees.
A curious, Eastern fragrance fills the breeze
From the ruinous Temple garden where roses are.

I dream of the rose-like perfume that fills your hair,
Of times when my lips were free
of your soft closed eyes,
While down in the tank the waters ripple and rise
And the flying foxes silently cleave the air.

The present is subtly welded into the past,
My love of you with the purple Indian dusk,
With its clinging scent of sandal incense and musk,
And withering jasmin flowers.

Reverie of Mahomed Akram

My eyes grow dim and my senses fail at last,
While the lonely hours
Follow each other, silently, one by one,
Till the night is almost done.
Then weary, and drunk with dreams,
with my garments damp
And heavy with dew, I wander towards the camp.
Tired, with a brain in which fancy
and fact are blent
I stumble across the ropes till I reach my tent.
And then to rest. To ensweeten my sleep with lies
To dream I lie in the light of your long lost eyes,
My lips set free,
To love and linger over your soft loose hair—
To dream I lay your delicate beauty bare
To solace my fevered eyes.
Ah,—if my life might end in a night like this—
Drift into death from dreams of your granted kiss !

VERSES

YOU ARE MY GOD,
and I would fain adore You
With sweet and secret rites of other days.
Burn scented oil in silver lamps before You,
Pour perfume on Your feet with prayer and praise.

Yet are we one; Your gracious condescension
Granted, and grants, the loveliness I crave.
One, in the perfect sense of Eastern mention,
" Gold and the Bracelet, Water and the Wave."

SONG OF KHAN ZADA

AS ONE MAY SIP
a stranger's bowl
You gave yourself but not your soul.
I wonder, now that time has passed,
Where you will come to rest at last.

You gave your beauty for an hour,
I held it gently as a flower.
You wished to leave me, told me so,—
I kissed your feet and let you go.

THE TEAK FOREST

WHETHER I LOVED YOU
who shall say ?
Whether I drifted down your way
In the endless River of Chance & Change,
And you woke the strange
Unknown longings that have no names,
But burn us all in their hidden flames,
Who shall say ?

Life is a strange and a wayward thing:
We heard the bells of the Temples ring,
The married children, in passing, sing.
The month of marriage, the month of spring,
Was full of the breath of sunburnt flowers
That bloom in a fiercer light than ours,
And, under a sky more fiercely blue,
I came to you !

You told me tales of your vivid life
Where death was cruel and danger rife—
Of deep dark forests, of poisoned trees,
Of pains and passions that scorch and freeze,
Of southern noontides and eastern nights,
Where love grew frantic with strange delights,
While men were slaying and maidens danced,
Till I, who listened, lay still, entranced.
Then, swift as a swallow heading south,
I kissed your mouth !

One night when the plains were
bathed in blood
From sunset light in a crimson flood,
We wandered under the young teak trees
Whose branches whined in the
light night breeze;
You led me down to the water's brink,
" The Spring where the Panthers come to drink
At night; there is always water here
Be the season never so parched and sere."
Have we souls of beast in the forms of men ?
I fain would have tasted your life-blood then.

The night fell swiftly; this sudden land
Can never lend us a twilight strand
'Twixt the daylight shore and the ocean night,
But takes—as it gives—at once, the light.
We laid us down on the steep hillside,
While far below us wild peacocks cried,
And we sometimes heard,
in the sunburnt grass,
The stealthy steps of the Jungle pass.
We listened; knew not whether they went
On love or hunger the more intent.
And under your kisses I hardly knew
Whether I loved or hated you.

But your words were flame and your kisses fire,
And who shall resist a strong desire ?
Not I, whose life is a broken boat
On a sea of passions, adrift, afloat.

And, whether I came in love or hate,
That I came to you was written by Fate
In every hue of the blood-red sky,
In every tone of the peacocks' cry.

While every gust of the Jungle night
Was fanning the flame you had set alight.
For these things have power to stir the blood
And compel us all to their own chance mood.
And to love or not we are no more free
Than a ripple to rise and leave the sea.

We are ever and always slaves of these,
Of the suns that scorch and the winds that freeze,
Of the faint sweet scents of the sultry air,
Of the half heard howl from the far off lair.
These chance things master us ever. Compel
To the heights of Heaven, the depths of Hell.

Whether I love you ? You do not ask,
Nor waste yourself on the thankless task.
I give your kisses at least return,
What matter whether they freeze or burn.
I feel the strength of your fervent arms,
What matter whether it heals or harms.

You are wise; you take what the Gods have sent.
You ask no questions, but rest content.
So I am with you to take your kiss,

And perhaps I value you more for this.
For this is Wisdom; to love, to live,
To take what Fate, or the Gods, may give,
To ask no question, to make no prayer,
To kiss the lips and caress the hair,
Speed passion's ebb as you greet its flow,—
To have,—to hold,—and,—in time,—let go !

And this is our Wisdom: we rest together
On the great lone hills in the storm-filled weather,
And watch the skies as they pale and burn,
The golden stars in their orbits turn.
While Love is with us, and Time and Peace,
And life has nothing to give but these.
But, whether you love me, who shall say,
Or whether you, drifting down my way
In the great sad River of Chance and Change,
With your looks so weary and words so strange,
Lit my soul from some hidden flame
To a passionate longing without a name,
Who shall say ?
Not I, who am but a broken boat,
Content for awhile to drift afloat
In the little noontide of love's delights
Between two Nights.

VALGOVIND'S BOAT SONG

WATERS GLISTEN
and sunbeams quiver,
The wind blows fresh and free.
Take my boat to your breast,
Oh, River ! Carry me out to Sea !

This land is laden with fruit and grain
With never a place left free for flowers,
A fruitful mother; but I am fain
For brides in their early bridal hours.

Take my boat to your breast, Oh, River !
Carry me out to Sea !

The Sea, beloved by a thousand ships,
Is maiden ever, and fresh and free.
Ah, for the touch of her cool green lips,
Carry me out to Sea !

Take my boat to your breast, dear River,
And carry it out to Sea !

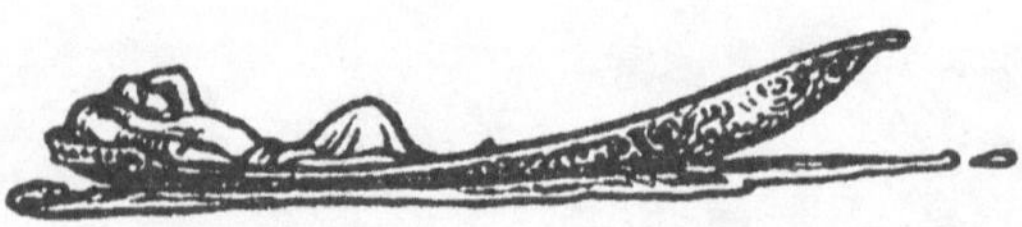

KASHMIRI SONG BY JUMA

YOU NEVER LOVED ME,
    and yet to save me,
One unforgettable night you gave me
Such chill embraces as
    the snow-covered heights
Receive from clouds, in northern, Auroral nights.
Such keen communion as the frozen mere
Has with immaculate moonlight, cold and clear.
And all desire,
Like failing fire,
Died slowly, faded surely, and sank to rest
Against the delicate chillness of your breast.

ZIRA: IN CAPTIVITY

LOVE ME A LITTLE, LORD, OR LET ME GO,
I am so weary walking to and fro
Through all your lonely halls
that were so sweet
Did they but echo to your coming feet.

When by the flowered scrolls of lace-like stone
Our women's windows—I am left alone,
Across the yellow Desert, looking forth,
I see the purple hills towards the north.

Behind those jagged Mountains' lilac crest
Once lay the captive bird's small rifled nest.
There was my brother slain, my sister bound;
His blood, her tears, drunk by the thirsty ground.

Then, while the burning village smoked on high,
And desecrated all the peaceful sky,
They took us captive, us, born frank and free,
On fleet, strong camels through the sandy sea.

Yet, when we rested, night-times on the sand
By the rare waters of this weary land,
Our captors, ere the camp was wrapped in sleep,
Talked, and I listened, and forgot to weep.

" Is he not brave and fair ? " they asked, " our King,
Slender as one tall palm-tree by a spring;

Erect, serene, with gravely brilliant eyes,
As deeply dark as are these desert skies.

" Truly no bitter fate," they said, and smiled,
" Awaits the beauty of this captured child ! "
Then something in my heart began to sing,
And secretly I longed to see the king.

Sometimes the other maidens sat in tears,
Sometimes, consoled, they jested at their fears,
Musing what lovers Time to them would bring;
But I was silent, thinking of the King.

Till, when the weary endless sands were passed,
When, far to south, the city rose at last,
All speech forsook me and my eyelids fell,
Since I already loved my Lord so well.

Then the division: some were sent away
To merchants in the city; some, they say,
To summer palaces, beyond the walls.
But me they took straight to the Sultan's halls.

Every morning I would wake and say:
" Ah, sisters, shall I see our Lord to-day ? "
The women robed me, perfumed me, and smiled;
" When were his feet unfleet to pleasure, child ? "

And tales they told me of his deeds in war
Of how his name was reverenced afar;

And, crouching closer in the lamp's faint glow,
They told me of his beauty, speaking low.

What need, what need ? the women wasted art;
I love you with every fibre of my heart
Already. My God ! when did I not love you,
In life, in death, when shall I not love you ?

You never seek me. All day long I lie
Watching the changes of the far-off sky
Behind the lattice-work of carven stone.
And all night long, alas ! I lie alone.

But you come never. Ah, my Lord the King,
How can you find it well to do this thing ?
Come once, come only: sometimes, as I lie,
I doubt if I shall see you first, or die.

Ah, could I hear your footsteps at the door
Hallow the lintel and caress the floor,
Then I might drink your beauty, satisfied,
Die of delight, ere you could reach my side.

Alas, you come not, Lord; life's flame burns low,
Faint for a loveliness it may not know,
Faint for your face,
                Oh, come—come soon to me—
Lest, though you should not,
                Death should, set me free !

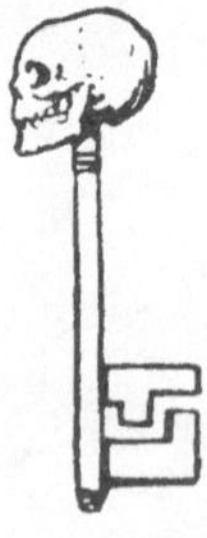

MARRIAGE THOUGHTS: BY MORSELLIN KHAN

BRIDEGROOM

I GIVE YOU MY HOUSE AND MY LANDS,
all golden with harvest;
My sword, my shield and my jewels,
the spoils of my strife,
My strength and my dreams,
and aught I have gathered of glory,
And to-night—to-night, I shall give you my very life.

BRIDE

I may not raise my eyes, oh my Lord, towards you,
And I may not speak: what matter ? my voice would fail.
But through my downcast lashes, feeling your beauty,
I shiver and burn with pleasure beneath my veil.

YOUNGER SISTERS

We throw sweet perfume upon her head,
And delicate flowers round her bed.
Ah, would that it were our turn to wed !

MOTHER

I see my daughter, vaguely, through my tears,
(Ah, lost caresses of my early years !)
I see the bridegroom, King of men in truth !
(Ah, my first lover, and my vanished youth !)

BRIDE

Almost I dread this night. My senses fail me.
How shall I dare to clasp a thing so dear ?

Marriage Thoughts

Many have feared your name, but I your beauty
Lord of my life, be gentle to my fear !

YOUNGER SISTERS.
In the softest silk is our sister dressed,
With silver and rubies upon her breast,
Where a dearer treasure to-night will rest.

DANCING GIRLS.
See ! his hair is like silk, and his teeth are whiter
Than whitest of jasmin flowers. Pity they marry him thus.
I would change my jewels against his caresses.
Verily, sisters, this marriage is greatly a loss to us !

BRIDE.
Would that the music ceased and the night drew round us,
With solitude, shadow, and sound of closing doors,
So that our lips might meet and our beings mingle,
While mine drank deep of the essence, beloved, of yours.

PASSING MENDICANT.
Out of the joy of your marriage feast,
Oh, brothers, be good to me.
The way is long and the Shrine is far,
Where my weary feet would be.

And feasting is always somewhat sad
To those outside the door—
Still; Love is only a dream, and Life
Itself is hardly more !

TO THE UNATTAINABLE: LAMENT OF MAHOMED AKRAM

I WOULD HAVE TAKEN GOLDEN STARS
from the sky for your necklace,
I would have shaken rose-leaves for your rest
from all the rose-trees.

But you had no need; the short sweet grass
sufficed for your slumber,
And you took no heed of such trifles
as gold or a necklace.

There is an hour, at twilight, too heavy with memory.
There is a flower that I fear, for your hair had its fragrance.

I would have squandered Youth for you,
and its hope and its promise,
Before you wandered, careless, away from
my useless passion.

But what is the use of my speech,
since I know of no words to recall you ?
I am praying that Time may teach, you,
your Cruelty, me, Forgetfulness.

MAHOMED AKRAM'S APPEAL TO THE STARS

OH, SILVER STARS THAT SHINE
on what I love,
Touch the soft hair and sparkle
in the eyes,—
Send, from your calm serenity above,
Sleep to whom, sleepless, here, despairing lies.

Broken, forlorn, upon the Desert sand
That sucks these tears, and utterly abased,
Looking across the lonely, level land,
With thoughts more desolate than any waste.

Planets that shine on what I so adore,
Now thrown, the hour is late, in careless rest,
Protect that sleep, which I may watch no more,
I, the cast out, dismissed and dispossessed.

Far in the hillside camp, in slumber lies
What my worn eyes worship but never see.
Happier Stars ! your myriad silver eyes
Feast on the quiet face denied to me.

Loved with a love beyond all words or sense,
Lost with a grief beyond the saltest tear,
So lovely, so removed, remote, and hence
So doubly and so desperately dear !

Mahomed Akram's Appeal to the Stars

Stars ! from your skies so purple and so calm,
That through the centuries your secrets keep,
Send to this worn-out brain some Occult Balm,
Send me, for many nights so sleepless, sleep.

And ere the sunshine of the Desert jars
My sense with sorrow and another day,
Through your soft Magic, oh, my Silver Stars !
Turn sleep to Death in some mysterious way.

REMINISCENCE OF MAHOMED AKRAM

I SHALL NEVER FORGET YOU, NEVER.
Never escape
Your memory woven about
the beautiful things of life.
The sudden Thought of your Face is like a Wound
When it comes unsought
On some scent of Jasmin, Lilies, or pale Tuberose,
Any one of the sweet white fragrant flowers,
Flowers I used to love and lay in your hair.

Sunset is terribly sad. I saw you stand
Tall against the red and the gold
like a slender palm;
The light wind stirred your hair
as you waved your hand,
Waved farewell, as ever, serene and calm,
To me, the passion-wearied and tost and torn,
Riding down the road in the gathering grey.
Since that day
The sunset red is empty, the gold forlorn.

Often across the Banqueting board at nights
Men linger about your name in careless praise—
The name that cuts deep into my soul like a knife;
And the gay guest-faces and flowers
and leaves and lights
Fade away from the failing sense in a haze,
And the music sways
Far away in unmeasured distance . . .

Less than the Dust

Zira: In Captivity

To the Unattainable: Lament of Mahomed Akram

Reminiscence of Mahomed Akram

Reminiscence of Mahomen Akram

I cannot forget—
I cannot escape.
What are the Stars to me ?
Stars that meant so much, too much,
in my youth:
Stars that sparkled about your eyes,
Made a radiance round your hair,
What are they now ?

Lingering lights of a Finished Feast,
Little lingering sparks rather,
Of a Light that is long gone out.

STORY BY LALLA-JI, THE PRIEST

HE LOVED THE PLANT WITH
a keen delight,
A passionate fervour, strange to see,
Tended it ardently, day and night,
Yet never a flower lit up the tree.

The leaves were succulent, thick, and green,
And, sessile, out of the snakelike stem
Rose spine-like fingers, alert and keen,
To catch at aught that molested them.

But though they nurtured it day and night,
With love and labour, the child and he
Were never granted the longed-for sight
Of a flower crowning the twisted tree.

Until one evening a wayworn Priest
Stopped for the night in the Temple shade
And shared the fare of their simple feast
Under the vines and the jasmin laid.

He, later, wandering round the flowers
Paused awhile by the blossomless tree.
The man said: " May it be fault of ours,
That never its buds my eyes may see ?

" A slip it came from the further East
Many a sunlit summer ago."
" It grows in our Jungles," said the Priest,
" Men see it rarely; but this I know,

Story by Lalla-ji, the Priest

" The Jungle people worship it; say
They bury a child around its roots—
Bury it living:—the only way
To crimson glory of flowers and fruits."

He spoke in whispers; his furtive glance
Probing the depths of the garden shade.
The man came closer, with eyes askance,
The child beside them shivered, afraid.

A cold wind drifted about the three,
Jarring the spines with a hungry sound,
The spines that grew on the snakelike tree
And guarded its roots beneath the ground.

After the fall of the summer rain
The plant was glorious, redly gay
Blood-red with blossom. Never again
Men saw the child in the Temple play.

REQUEST

GIVE ME YOURSELF ONE HOUR;
I do not crave
For any love, or even thought, of me.
Come, as a Sultan may caress a slave
And then forget for ever, utterly.

Come! as west winds, that passing, cool and wet,
O'er desert places, leave them fields in flower;
And all my life, for I shall not forget,
Will keep the fragrance of that perfect hour !

STORY OF UDAIPORE: TOLD BY LALLA-JI, THE PRIEST

AND WHEN THE SUMMER HEAT IS GREAT,
AND EVERY HOUR INTENSE,
THE MOGHRA, WITH IS SUBTLE FLOWERS,
INTOXICATES THE SENSE.

The Coco palms stood tall and slim, against the golden glow,
And all their grey and graceful plumes were waving
to and fro.

She lay forgetful in the boat, and watched the dying Sun
Sink slowly lakewards, while the stars replaced him,
one by one.

She saw the marble Temple walls long white
reflections make,
The echoes of their silver bells were blown across the lake.

The evening air was very sweet; from off the island bowers
Came scents of Moghra trees in bloom,
and Oleander flowers.

" The Moghra flowers that smell so sweet
When love's young fancies play;
The acrid Moghra flowers, still sweet
Though love be burnt away."

The boat went drifting, uncontrolled,
the rower rowed no more,
But deftly turned the slender prow towards the further shore.

The dying sunset touched with gold the Jasmin in his hair;
His eyes were darkly luminous: she looked
and found him fair.

And so persuasively he spoke, she could not say him nay,
And when his young hands took her own,
she smiled & let them stay.

And all the youth awake in him, all love of Love in her,
All scents of white and subtle flowers that filled
the twilight air

Combined together with the night in kind conspiracy
To do Love service, while the boat went
drifting onwards, free.

" The Moghra flowers, the Moghra flowers,
While Youth's quick pulses play
They are so sweet, they still are sweet,
Though passion burns away."

Low in the boat the lovers lay, and from his sable curls
The Jasmin flowers slipped away to rest among the girl's.

Oh, silver lake and silver night and tender silver sky !
Where as the hours passed, the moon rose white
& cold on high.

" The Moghra flowers, the Moghra flowers,
So dear to Youth at play;
The small and subtle Moghra flowers
That only last a day."

Suddenly, frightened, she awoke, and waking vaguely saw
The boat had stranded in the sedge
that fringed the further shore.

The breeze grown chilly, swayed the palms; she heard,
still half awake,
A prowling jackal's hungry cry blown faintly o'er the lake.

She shivered, but she turned to kiss his soft,
remembered face,
Lit by the pallid light he lay, in Youth's abandoned grace.

But as her lips met his she paused, in terror and dismay,
The white moon showed her by her side
asleep a Leper lay.

" Ah Moghra flowers,
white Moghra flowers,
All love is blind, they say;
The Moghra flowers,
so sweet, so sweet,
Though love be burnt away ! "

VALGOVIND'S SONG IN THE SPRING

THE TEMPLE BELLS ARE RINGING,
The young green corn is springing,
And the marriage month is drawing very near.
I lie hidden in the grass,
And I count the moments pass,
For the month of marriages is drawing near.

Soon, ah, soon, the women spread
The appointed bridal bed
With hibiscus buds and crimson marriage flowers,
Where, when all the songs are done,
And the dear dark night begun,
I shall hold her in my happy arms for hours.

She is young and very sweet,
From the silver on her feet
To the silver and the flowers in her hair,
And her beauty makes me swoon,
As the Moghra trees at noon
Intoxicate the hot and quivering air.

Ah, I would the hours were fleet
As her silver circled feet.
I am weary of the daytime and the night
I am weary unto death,
Oh my rose with jasmin breath,
With this longing for your beauty and your light.

YOUTH

I AM NOT SURE IF I KNEW
the truth
What his case or crime might be,
I only know that he pleaded Youth,
A beautiful, golden plea !

Youth, with its sunlit, passionate eyes,
Its roseate velvet skin—
A plea to cancel a thousand lies,
Or a thousand nights of sin.

The men who judged him were old and grey,
Their eyes and their senses dim,
He brought the light of a warm Spring day
To the Court-house bare and grim.

Could he plead in a lovelier way ?
His judges acquitted him.

WHEN LOVE IS OVER: SONG OF KHAN ZADA

ONLY IN AUGUST MY HEART
was aflame,
Catching the scent of your
Wind-stirred hair,
Now, though you spread it
to soften my sleep
Through the night, I should hardly care.

Only last August I drank that water
Because it had chanced to cool your hands;
When love is over, how little of love
Even the lover understands !

GOLDEN EYES

OH AMBER EYES,
Oh Golden Eyes
Oh Eyes so softly gay !
Wherein swift fancies fall and rise,
Grow dark and fade away.
Eyes like a little limpid pool
That holds a sunset sky,
While on its surface, calm and cool,
Blue water lilies lie.

Oh Tender Eyes, oh Wistful Eyes,
You smiled on me one day,
And all my life, in glad surprise,
Leapt up and pleaded " Stay ! "
Alas, oh cruel, starlike eyes,
So grave and yet so gay,
You went to lighten other skies,
Smiled once and passed away.

Oh, you whom I name " Golden Eyes,"
Perhaps I used to know
Your beauty under other skies
In lives lived long ago.
Perhaps I rowed with galley slaves,
Whose labour never ceased,
To bring across Phoenician waves
Your treasure from the East.

Golden Eyes

Maybe you were an Emperor then
And I a favourite slave;
Some youth, whom from the lions' den
You vainly tried to save !
Maybe I reigned, a mighty King,
The early nations knew,
And you were some slight captive thing,
Some maiden whom I slew.

Perhaps, adrift on desert shores
Beside some shipwrecked prow,
I gladly gave my life for yours.
Would I might give it now !
Or on some sacrificial stone
Strange Gods we satisfied,
Perhaps you stooped and left a throne
To kiss me ere I died.

Perhaps, still further back than this,
In times ere men were men,
You granted me a moment's bliss
In some dark desert den,
When, with your amber eyes alight
With iridescent flame
And fierce desire for love's delight,
Towards my lair you came.

Ah laughing, ever-brilliant eyes,
These things men may not know,
But something in your radiance lies,

That, centuries ago,
Lit up my life in one wild blaze
Of infinite desire
To revel in your golden rays,
Or in your light expire.

If this, oh Strange Ringed Eyes, be true
That through all changing lives
This longing love I have for you
Eternally survives,
May I not sometimes dare to dream
In some far time to be
Your softly golden eyes may gleam
Responsively on me ?

Ah gentle, subtly changing eyes,
You smiled on me one day,
And all my life in glad surprise
Leaped up, imploring " Stay ! "
Alas, alas, oh Golden Eyes,
So cruel and so gay,
You went to shine in other skies,
Smiled once and passed away.

KOTRI, BY THE RIVER

AT KOTRI, BY THE RIVER, WHEN EVENING'S
sun is low,
The waving palm trees quiver,
the golden waters low,
The shining ripples shiver, descending to the sea.
At Kotri, by the river, she used to wait for me.

So pale, so young, so slender, she was, with wistful eyes
As luminous and tender as Kotri's twilight skies.
Her face broke into flowers, red flowers at the mouth,
Her voice,—she sang for hours like bulbuls in the south.

We sat beside the water through burning summer days,
And many things I taught her of Life and all its ways.
Of Love, man's loveliest duty, of Passion's reckless pain,
Of Youth, whose transient beauty comes once,
but not again.

She lay and laughed and listened beside the water's edge.
The glancing river glistened and glinted through the sedge.
Green parrots flew above her and, as the daylight died,
Her young arms drew her lover more closely to her side.

Oh days so warm and golden ! oh nights so cool and still !
When Love would not be holden, and Pleasure
had his will.
Days when in after leisure, content to rest we lay,
Nights, when her lips' soft pressure drained
all my life away.

And while we sat together, beneath the Babul trees,
The fragrant, sultry weather cooled by the river breeze,
If passion faltered ever, and left the senses free,
We heard the tireless river descending to the sea.

I know not where she wandered, or went in after days,
Or if her youth was squandered in Love's
        more doubtful ways.
Perhaps, beside the river she died, still young and fair;
Perchance the grasses quiver above her slumber there.

At Kotri, by the river, maybe I too shall sleep
The sleep that lasts for ever, too deep for dreams;
        too deep.
Maybe among the shingle and sand of floods to be
Her dust and mine may mingle and float away to sea.

Ah Kotri, by the river, when evening's sun is low,
Your faint reflections quiver, your golden ripples glow.
You knew, oh Kotri river, that love which
        could not last.
For me your palms still shiver with passions of the past.

FAREWELL

FAREWELL, AZIZ, IT WAS NOT MINE
to fold you
Against my heart for any length of days.
I had no loveliness, alas, to hold you,
No siren voice, no charm that lovers praise.

Yet, in the midst of grief and desolation,
Solace I my despairing soul with this:
Once, for my life's eternal consolation,
You lent my lips your loveliness to kiss.

Ah, that one night ! I think Love's very essence
Distilled itself from out my joy and pain,
Like tropical trees, whose fervid inflorescence
Glows, gleams and dies, never to bloom again.

Often I marvel how I met the morning
With living eyes, after that night with you,
Ah, how I cursed the wan, white light for dawning,
And mourned the paling stars, as each withdrew !

Yet I, even I, who am less than dust before you,
Less than the lowest lintel of your door,
Was given one breathless midnight, to adore you.
Fate, having granted this, can give no more !

AFRIDI LOVE

SINCE, OH, BELOVED,
you are not even faithful
To me, who loved you so, for one short night,
For one brief space of darkness,
though my absence
Did but endure until the dawning light.

Since all your beauty—which was mine—
you squandered
On that which now lies dead across your door;
See here this knife, made keen and
bright to kill you.
You shall not see the sun rise any more.

Lie still ! Lie still ! In all the empty village
Who is there left to hear or heed your cry ?
All are gone down to labour in the valley,
Who will return before your time to die ?

No use to struggle; when I found you sleeping,
I took your hands and bound them to your side,
And both these slender feet, too apt at straying,
Down to the cot on which you lie are tied.

Afridi Love

Lie still, Beloved; that dead thing lying yonder,
I hated and I killed, but love is sweet,
And you are more than sweet to me, who love you,
Who decked my eyes with dust from off your feet.

Give me your lips; Ah, lovely and disloyal
Give me yourself again; before you go
Down through the darkness of the Great, Blind Portal,
All of life's best and basest you must know.

Erstwhile Beloved, you were so young and fragile
I held you gently, as one holds a flower:
But now, God knows, what use to still be tender
To one whose life is done within an hour ?

I hurt ? What then ?
Death will not hurt you, dearest,
As you hurt me, just for a single night,
You call me cruel, who laid my life in ruins
To gain one little moment of delight.

Look up, look out, across the open doorway
The sunlight streams. The distant hills are blue.
Look at the pale, pink peach trees in our garden,
Sweet fruit will come of them;—but not for you.

The fair, far snow, upon those jagged mountains
That gnaw against the hard blue Afghan sky
Will soon descend, set free by summer sunshine.
You will not see those torrents sweeping by.

Afridi
Love

The world is not for you. From this day forward,
You must lie still alone; who would not lie
Alone for one night only, though returning
I was, when earliest dawn should break the sky.

There lies my lute, and many strings are broken,
Some one was playing it, and some one tore
The silken tassels round my Hookah woven;
Some one who plays & smokes, & loves, no more !

Some one who took last night his fill of pleasure,
As I took mine at dawn ! The knife went home
Straight through his heart !
God only knows my rapture
Bathing my chill hands in the warm red foam.

And so I pain you ? This is only loving,
Wait till I kill you ! Ah, this soft, curled hair !
Surely the fault was mine, to love and leave you
Even a single night, you are so fair.

Cold steel is very cooling to the fervour
Of over passionate ones, Beloved, like you.
Nay, turn your lips to mine. Not quite unlovely
They are as yet, as yet, though quite untrue.

What will your brother say, to-night returning
With laden camels homewards to the hills,
Finding you dead, and me asleep beside you.
Will he awake me first before he kills ?

Afridi Love

For I shall sleep. Here on the cot beside you
When you, my Heart's Delight, are cold in death.
When your young heart and restless lips are silent,
Grown chilly, even beneath my burning breath.

When I have slowly drawn my knife across you,
Taking my pleasure as I see you swoon,
I shall sleep sound, worn out by love's last fervour,
And then, God grant your kinsmen kill me soon !

YASMINI

AT NIGHT, WHEN PASSION'S
ebbing tide
Left bare the Sands of Truth,
Yasmini, resting by my side,
Spoke softly of her youth.

" And one," she said, " was tall and slim,
Two crimson rose leaves made his mouth
And I was fain to follow him
Down to his village in the South.

" He was to build a hut hard by
The stream where palms were growing,
We were to live, and love, and lie,
And watch the water flowing.

" Ah, dear, delusive, distant shore,
By dreams of futile fancy gilt !
The riverside we never saw,
The palm leaf hut was never built !

" One had a Tope of Mangoe trees,
Where early morning, noon and late,
The Persian wheels, with patient ease,
Brought up their liquid, silver freight.

" And he was fain to rise and reach
That garden sloping to the sea,
Whose groves along the wave-swept beach
Should shelter him and love and me.

" Doubtless, upon that western shore
With ripe fruit falling to the ground,
There dwells the Peace he hungered for,
The lovely Peace we never found.

" Then there came one with eager eyes
And keen sword, ready for the fray.
He missed the storms of Northern skies,
The reckless raid and skirmish gay !

" He rose from dreams of war's alarms,
To make his daggers keen and bright,
Desiring, in my very arms,
The fiercer rapture of the fight !

" He left me soon; too soon, and sought
The stronger, earlier love again.
News reached me from the Cabul Court,
Afterwards nothing; doubtless slain.

" Doubtless his brilliant, haggard eyes,
Long since took leave of life and light,
And those lithe limbs I used to prize
Feasted the jackal and the kite.

“ But the most loved ! his sixteen years
Shone in his cheeks’ transparent red.
My kisses were his first: my tears
Fell on his face when he was dead.

“ He died, he died, I speak the truth,
Though light love leave his memory dim,
He was the Lover of my Youth
And all my youth went down with him.

“ For passion ebbs and passion flows,
But under every new caress
The riven heart more keenly knows
Its own inviolate faithfulness.

“ Our Gods are kind and still deem fit
As in old days, with those to lie,
Whose silent hearths are yet unlit
By the soft light of infancy.

“ Therefore, one strange, mysterious night
Alone within theTemple shade,
Recipient of a God’s delight
I lay enraptured, unafraid.

“ Also to me the boon was given,
But mourning quickly followed mirth,
My son, whose father stooped from Heaven,
Died in the moment of his birth.

" When from the war beyond the seas
The reckless Lancers home returned,
Their spoils were laid across my knees
About my lips their kisses burned.

" Back from the Comradeship of Death,
Free from the Friendship of the Sword,
With brilliant eyes and famished breath
They came to me for their reward.

" Why do I tell you all these things,
Baring my life to you, unsought ?
When Passion folds his wearied wings
Sleep should be follower, never Thought.

" Ay, let us sleep. The window pane
Grows pale against the purple sky.
The dawn is with us once again,
The dawn; which always means good-bye."

Within her little trellised room,
beside the palm-fringed sea,
She wakeful in the scented gloom,
spoke of her youth to me.

OJIRA, TO HER LOVER

I AM WAITING IN THE DESERT, LOOKING OUT
towards the sunset,
And counting every moment till we meet.
I am waiting by the marshes and I tremble and I listen
Till the soft sands thrill beneath your coming feet.

Till I see you, tall and slender, standing clear
against the skyline
A graceful shade across the lingering red,
While your hair the breezes ruffle, turns to silver
in the twilight,
And makes a fair faint aureole round your head.

Far away towards the sunset I can see a narrow river
That unwinds itself in red tranquillity.
I can hear its rippled meeting, and the gurgle of its greeting,
As it mingles with the loved and long sought sea.

In the purple sky above me showing dark against the starlight,
Long wavering flights of homeward birds fly low,
They cry each one to the other, and their weird
and wistful calling,
Makes most melancholy music as they go.

Oh, my dearest hasten, hasten ! It is lonely here. Already
Have I heard the jackals' first assembling cry,
And among the purple shadows of the mangroves
and the marshes
Fitful echoes of their footfalls passing by.

Ojira, to her Lover

Ah, come soon ! my arms are empty, and so weary
for your beauty,
I am thirsty for the music of your voice.
Come to make the marshes joyous with the sweetness
of your presence
Let your nearing feet bid all the sands rejoice !

My hands, my lips are feverish with the longing
and the waiting
And no softness of the twilight soothes their heat,
Till I see your radiant eyes, shining stars
beneath the starlight,
Till I kiss the slender coolness of your feet.

Ah, loveliest, most reluctant, when you lay yourself
beside me,
All the planets reel around me—fade away,
And the sands grow dim, uncertain,—I stretch out
my hands towards you
While I try to speak but know not what I say !

I am faint with love and longing and my burning eyes
are gazing
Where the furtive Jackals wage their famished strife,
Oh, your shadow on the mangroves ! and your step
upon the sandhills,—
This is the loveliest evening of my life !

THOUGHTS: MAHOMED AKRAM

IF SOME DAY THIS BODY OF MINE
were burned
(It found no favour alas ! with you)
And the ashes scattered abroad, unurned,
Would Love die also, would Thought die too ?
But who can answer, or who can trust,
No dreams would harry the windblown dust ?

Were I laid away in the furrows deep
Secure from jackal and passing plough,
Would your eyes not follow me still through sleep
Torment me then as they torture now ?
Would you ever have loved me, Golden Eyes,
Had I done aught better or otherwise ?

Was I overspeechful, or did you yearn
When I sat silent, for songs or speech ?
Ah, Beloved, I had been so apt to learn,
So apt, had you only cared to teach.
But time for silence and song is done,
You wanted nothing, my Golden Sun !

What should you want of a waning star ?
That drifts in its lonely orbit far
Away from your soft, effulgent light
In outer planes of Eternal night ?

PRAYER

YOU ARE ALL THAT IS
lovely and light,
Aziz whom I adore,
And, waking, after the night,
I am weary with dreams of you.
Every nerve in my heart is terse and sore
As I rise to another morning
apart from you.

I dream of your luminous eyes,
Aziz whom I adore !
Of the ruffled silk of your hair,
I dream, and the dreams are lies.
But I love them, knowing no more,
Will ever be mine of you
Aziz, my life's despair.

I would burn for a thousand days,
Aziz whom I adore,
Be tortured, slain, in unheard of ways
If you pitied the pain I bore.
You pity ! Your bright eyes,
fastened on other things,
Are keener to sting my soul,
than scorpion stings !

Prayer

You are all that is lovely to me,
All that is light,
One white rose in a Desert of weariness.

I only live in the night,
The night, with its fair false dreams of you,
You and your loveliness.

Give me your love for a day,
A night, an hour:
If the wages of sin are Death
I am willing to pay.
What is my life but a breath
Of passion burning away ?
Away for an unplucked flower.
Oh, Aziz whom I adore,
Aziz my one delight,
Only one night, I will die before day,
And trouble your life no more.

THE ALOE

MY LIFE WAS LIKE AN ALOE FLOWER,
beneath an orient sky,
Your sunshine touched it for an hour;
it blossomed but to die.

Torn up, cast out, on rubbish heaps where
red flames work their will
Each atom of the Aloe keeps the
flower-time fragrance still.

MEMORY

HOW I LOVED YOU IN YOUR SLEEP
With the starlight on your hair !

The touch of your lips was sweet,
Aziz whom I adore,
I lay at your slender feet,
And against their soft palms pressed,
I fitted my face to rest.
As winds blow over the sea
From Citron gardens ashore,
Came, through your scented hair,
The breeze of the night to me.

My lips grew arid and dry,
My nerves were tense,
Though your beauty soothe the eye
It maddens the sense.
Every curve of that beauty is known to me,
Every tint of that delicate roseleaf skin,
And these are printed on every atom of me,
Burnt in on every fibre until I die,
And for this, my sin,
I doubt if ever, though dust I be,
The dust will lose the desire,
The torment and hidden fire,
Of my passionate love for you,
Aziz whom I adore,

Memory

My dust will be full of your beauty, as is the blue
And infinite ocean full of the azure sky.

In the light that waxed and waned
Playing about your slumber in silver bars,
As the palm trees swung their feathery fronds
athwart the star
How quiet and young you were,
Pale as the Champa flowers, violet veined
That sweet and fading, lay in your loosened hair.

How sweet you were in your sleep,
With the starlight on your hair !
Your throat thrown backwards, bare,
And touched with circling moonbeams
silver white
On the couch's sombre shade,
Oh, Aziz my one delight,
When Youth's passionate pulses fade,
And his golden heart beats slow,
When across the infinite sky
I see the roseate glow
Of my last, last sunset flare,
I shall send my thoughts to this night
And remember you as I die,
The one thing among all the things
of this world found fair,

How sweet you were in your sleep,
With the starlight, silver and sable,
across your hair !

Valgovind's Song in the Spring

Ojira, to her Lover

Deserted Gipsy's Song : Hillside Camp

The Garden by the Bridge

THE FIRST LOVER

AS O'ER THE VESSEL'S SIDE SHE LEANT,
She saw the swimmer in the sea
With eager eyes on her intent,
" Come down, come down
and swim with me."

So weary was she of her lot,
Tired of the ship's monotony,
She straightway all the world forgot
Save the young swimmer in the sea.

So when the dusky, dying light
Left all the water dark and dim,
She softly in the friendly night
Slipped down the vessel's side to him.

Intent and brilliant, brightly dark,
She saw his burning, eager eyes,
And many a phosphorescent spark
About his shoulders fall and rise.

As through the hushed and Eastern night
They swam together, hand in hand,
Or lay and laughed in sheer delight
Full length upon the level sand.

" Ah, soft, delusive, purple night
Whose darkness knew no vexing moon !
Ah, cruel, needless, dawning light
That trembles in the sky too soon ! "

KHAN ZADA'S SONG ON THE HILLSIDE

THE FIRES THAT BURN ON
all the hills
Light up the landscape grey,
The arid desert land distils
The fervours of the day.

The clear white moon sails
through the skies
And silvers all the night,
I see the brilliance of your eyes
And need no other light.

The death sighs of a thousand flowers
The fervent day has slain
Are wafted through the twilight hours,
And perfume all the plain.

My senses strain, and try to clasp
Their sweetness in the air,
In vain, in vain; they only grasp
The fragrance of your hair.

The plain is endless space expressed;
Vast is the sky above,
I only feel, against your breast,
Infinities of love.

DESERTED GIPSY'S SONG: HILLSIDE CAMP

"SHE IS GLAD TO RECEIVE
your turquoise ring,
Dear and dark-eyed Lover of mine !
I, to have given you everything:
Beauty maddens the soul like Wine !

" She is proud to have held
aloof her charms,
Slender, dark-eyed Lover of mine !
But I, of the night you lay in my arms:
Beauty maddens the sense like Wine !

" She triumphs to think that your heart is won,
Stately, dark-eyed Lover of mine !
I had not a thought of myself, not one:
Beauty maddens the brain like Wine !

" She will speak you softly,
while skies are blue,
Dear, deluded Lover of mine !
I would lose both body and soul for you:
Beauty maddens the brain like Wine !

" While the ways are fair she will love you well,
Dear, disdainful Lover of mine !
But I would have followed you down to Hell:
Beauty maddens the soul like Wine !

Deserted Gipsy's Song: Hillside Camp

" Though you lay at her feet the days to be,
Now no longer Lover of mine !
You can give her naught that you gave not me:
Beauty maddened my soul like Wine !

" When the years have shown
what is false or true:
Beauty maddens the sight like Wine !
You will understand how I cared for you,
First and only Lover of mine ! "

THE PLAINS

HOW ONE LOVES THEM
these white horizons;
whether Desert or Sea,—
Vague and vast and infinite;
faintly clear—
Surely, hid in the far away,
unknown " There,"
Lie the things so longed for and found not,
found not, Here.

Only where some passionate, level land
Stretches itself in reaches of golden sand,
Only where the sea-line is joined
to the sky-line, clear,
Beyond the curve of ripple or white
foamed crest,—
Shall the weary eyes
Distressed by the broken skies,—
Broken by Minaret, mountain
or towering tree,—
Shall the weary eyes be assuaged,
—be assuaged,—and rest.

" LOST DELIGHT " : AFTER THE HAZARA WAR

LIE ALONE, BENEATH THE ALMOND BLOSSOMS,
Where we two lay together in the spring,
And now, as then, the mountain snows
are melting,
This year, as last, the water-courses sing.

That was another spring, and other flowers,
Hung, pink and fragile, on the leafless tree,
The land rejoiced in other running water,
And I rejoiced, because you were with me.

You, with your soft eyes, darkly lashed and shaded,
Your red lips like a living, laughing rose,
Your restless, amber limbs so lithe and slender
Now lost to me. Gone whither no man knows.

You lay beside me singing in the sunshine:
The rough, white fur, unloosened at the neck,
Showed the smooth skin, fair as the Almond blossoms,
On which the sun could find no flaw or fleck.

I lie alone, beneath the almond flowers,
I hated them to touch you as they fell,
And now, who killed you ?
worse, ah, worse, who loves you ?
(My soul is burning as men burn in Hell.)

“Lost Delight”: After the Hazara War

How I have sought you in the crowded cities !
I have been mad, they say, for many days.
I know not how I came here, to the valley,
What fate has led me, through what doubtful ways.

Somewhere I see my sword has done good service,
Some one I killed who, smiling, used your name,
But in what country ? Nay, I have forgotten,
All thought is shrivelled in my heart’s hot flame.

Where are you now, Delight, and where your beauty,
Your subtle curls, and laughing, changeful face?
Bound, bruised and naked
(dear God, grant me patience),
And sold in Cabul in the market-place.

I asked of you of all men. Who could tell me ?
Among so many captured, sold, or slain,
What fate was yours ? (ah, dear God, grant me patience,
My heart is burnt, is burnt, with fire and pain.)

Oh, lost Delight ! my heart is almost breaking,
My sword is broken and my feet are sore,
The people look at me and say in passing,
“ He will not leave the village any more.”

For as the evening falls, the fever rises,
With frantic thoughts careering through the brain,
Wild thoughts of you (ah, dear God, grant me patience,
My soul is hurt beyond all men call pain.)

“Lost Delight”: After the Hazara War

I lie alone, beneath the Almond blossoms,
And see the white snow melting on the hills
Till Khorassan is gay with water-courses,
Glad with the tinkling sound of running rills,

And well I know that when the fragile petals
Fall softly, e’er the first green leaves appear,
(Ah, for these last few days,
God grant me patience,)
Since Delight is not, I shall not be, here !

UNFORGOTTEN

DO YOU EVER THINK OF ME ?
you who died
Ere our Youth's first fervour chilled,
With your soft eyes closed and
your pulses stilled
Lying alone, aside,
Do you ever think of me, left in the light,
From the endless calm of your
dawnless night ?

I am faithful always: I do not say
That the lips which thrilled
to your lips of old
To lesser kisses are always cold;
Had you wished for this in its narrow sense
Our love perhaps had been less intense;
But as we held faithfulness, you and I,
I am faithful always, as you who lie,
Asleep for ever, beneath the grass,
While the days and nights and
the seasons pass,—
Pass away.

I keep your memory near my heart,
My brilliant, beautiful guiding Star,
Till long life over, I too depart
To the infinite night where perhaps you are.

Unfor-gotten

Oh, are you anywhere ? Loved so well !
I would rather know you alive in Hell
Than think your beauty is nothing now,
With its deep dark eyes and its tranquil brow
Where the hair fell softly. Can this be true
That nothing, nowhere, exists of you ?
Nothing, nowhere, oh, loved so well
I have never forgotten.
Do you still keep
Thoughts of me through your dreamless sleep ?

Oh, gone from me ! lost in Eternal Night,
Lost Star of light,
Risen splendidly, set so soon,
Through the weariness of life's afternoon
I dream of your memory yet.
My loved and lost, whom I could not save,
My youth went down with you to the grave,
Though other planets and stars may rise,
I dream of your soft and sorrowful eyes
And I cannot forget.

SONG OF FAIZ ULLA

JUST AT THE TIME WHEN JASMINS BLOOM,
most sweetly in the summer weather,
Lost in the scented Jungle gloom, one sultry night
we spent together,
We, Love and Night, together blent,
a Trinity of tranced content.

Yet, while your lips were wholly mine, to kiss,
to drink from, to caress,
We heard some far-off faint distress;
harsh drop of poison in sweet wine
Lessening the fullness of delight,
Some quivering note of human pain,
Which rose and fell and rose again,
in plaintive sobs throughout the night,

Spoiling the perfumed, moonless hours
We spent among the Jasmin flowers.

STORY OF LILAVANTI

THEY LAY THE SLENDER
body down
With all its wealth of wetted hair,
Only a daughter of the town,
But very young and slight and fair.

The eyes, whose light one cannot see,
Are sombre doubtless like the tresses,
The mouth's soft curvings seem to be
A roseate series of caresses.

And where the skin has all but dried
(The air is sultry in the room)
Upon her breast and either side,
It shows a soft and amber bloom.

By women here, who knew her life,
A leper husband, I am told,
Took all this loveliness to wife
When it was barely ten years old.

And when the child in shocked dismay
Fled from the hated husband's care
He caught and tied her, so they say,
Down to his bedside by her hair.

To some low quarter of the town,
Escaped a second time, she flew;
Her beauty brought her great renown
And many lovers here she knew,

When, as the mystic Eastern night
With purple shadow filled the air,
Behind her window framed in light,
She sat with jasmin in her hair.

At last she loved a youth, who chose
To keep this wild flower for his own,
He in his garden set his rose
Where it might bloom for him alone.

Cholera come; her lover died,
Want drove her to the streets again,
And women found her there, who tried
To turn her beauty into gain.

But she who in those garden ways
Had learnt of Love, would now no more
Be bartered in the market-place
For silver, as in days before.

That former life she strove to change;
She sold the silver off her arms,
While all the world grew cold and strange
To broken health and fading charms.

Till, finding lovers, but no friend
Nor any place to rest or hide,
She grew despairing at the end,
Slipped softly down a well and died.

And yet, how short, when all is said,
This little life of love and tears !
Her age, they say, beside her bed,
To-day is only fifteen years.

THE GARDEN BY THE BRIDGE

THE DESERT SANDS ARE HEATED,
parched and dreary,
The tigers rend alive their quivering prey
In the near Jungle; here the kites rise, weary,
Too gorged with living food to fly away.

All night the hungry jackals howl together
Over the carrion in the river bed,
Or seize some small soft thing of fur or feather
Whose dying shrieks on the night air are shed.

I hear from yonder Temple in the distance
Whose roof with obscene carven Gods is piled,
Reiterated with a sad insistence,
Sobs of, perhaps, some immolated child.

Strange rites here, where the archway's shade
is deeper
Are consummated in the river bed;
Parias steal the rotten railway sleeper
To burn the bodies of their cholera dead.

But yet, their lust, their hunger, cannot shame them
Goaded by fierce desire, that flays and stings;
Poor beasts, and poorer men.
Nay, who shall blame them ?
Blame the Inherent Cruelty of things.

The Garden by the Bridge

The world is horrible and I am lonely,
Let me rest here where yellow roses bloom
And find forgetfulness, remembering only
Your face beside me in the scented gloom.

Nay, do not shrink ! I am not here for passion,
I crave no love, only a little rest,
Although I would my face lay, lover's fashion.
Against the tender coolness of your breast.

I am so weary of the Curse of Living
The endless, aimless torture, tumult, fears.
Surely, if life were any God's free giving,
He, seeing His gift, long since went blind with tears.

Seeing us; our fruitless strife, our futile praying
Our luckless Present and our bloodstained past.
Poor players, who make a trick or two in playing,
But know that death must win the game at last.

As round the Fowler, with feathered slaughter
The little joyous lark, unconscious sings,—
As the pink Lotus floats on azure water,
Innocent of the mud from whence it springs.

You walk through life, unheeding all the sorrow,
The fear and pain set close around your way,
Meeting with hopeful eyes each gay to-morrow,
Loving with joy each hour of glad to-day.

The Garden by the Bridge

I love to have you thus (nay, dear, lie quiet,
How should these reverent fingers wrong your hair ?)
So calmly careless of the rush and riot
That rages round us seething everywhere.

You do not understand. You think your beauty
Does but inflame my senses to desire,
Till all you hold as loyalty and duty,
Is shrunk and shrivelled in the ardent fire.

You wrong me, wearied out with thought and grieving
As though the whole world's sorrow eat my heart,
I come to gaze upon your face believing
Its beauty is as ointment to the smart.

Lie still and let me in my desolation
Caress the soft loose hair a moment's span.
Since Loveliness is Life's one Consolation,
And love the only Lethe left to man.

Ah, give me here beneath the trees in flower,
Beside the river where the fireflies pass,
One little dusky, all consoling hour
Lost in the shadow of the long grown grass.

Give me, oh, you whose arms are soft and slender,
Whose eyes are nothing but one long caress,
Against your heart, so innocent and tender,
A little Love and some Forgetfulness.

FATE KNOWS NO TEARS

JUST AS THE DAWN OF LOVE
was breaking
Across the weary world of grey,
Just as my life once more was waking
As roses waken late in May,
Fate, blindly cruel and havoc-making,
Stepped in and carried you away.

Memories have I none in keeping
Of times I held you near my heart,
Of dreams when we were near to weeping
That dawn should bid us rise and part;
Never alas, I saw you sleeping
With soft closed eyes and lips apart

Breathing my name still through your dreaming.—
Ah ! had you stayed, such things had been !
But fate, unheeding human scheming,
Serenely reckless came between—
Fate with her cold eyes hard and gleaming
Unscared by all the sorrow seen.

Ah ! well-beloved, I never told you
I did not show in speech or song,
How at the end I longed to fold you
Close in my arms, so fierce and strong
The longing grew to have and hold you,
You, and you only, all life long.

They who know nothing call me fickle,
Keen to pursue and loth to keep.
Ah, could they see these tears that trickle
From eyes erstwhile too proud to weep.
Could see me, prone, beneath the sickle,
While pain and sorrow stand and reap !

Fate
Knows
No
Tears

Unopened scarce, yet overblown, lie
The hopes that rose-like round me grew,
The lights are low, and more than lonely
This life I lead apart from you.
Come back, come back ! I want you only,
And you who loved me never knew.

You loved me, pleaded for compassion
On all the pain I would not share;
And I in weary, halting fashion
Was loth to listen, long to care;
But now, dear God ! I faint with passion
For your far eyes and distant hair.

Yes, I am faint with love, and broken
With sleepless nights and empty days;
I want your soft words fiercely spoken,
Your tender looks and wayward ways—
Want that strange smile that gave me token
Of many things that no man says.

Cold was I, weary, slow to waken
Till, startled by your ardent eyes,

Fate Knows No Tears

I felt the soul within me shaken
And long-forgotten senses rise;
But in that moment you were taken,
And thus we lost our Paradise !

Farewell, we may not now recover
That golden " Then " misspent, passed by.
We shall not meet as loved and lover
Here, or hereafter, you and I.
My time for loving you is over,
Love has no future, but to die.

And thus we part, with no believing
In any chance of future years.
We have no idle self-deceiving,
No half-consoling hopes and fears;
We know the Gods grant no retrieving
A wasted chance. Fate knows no tears.

VERSES: FAIZ ULLA

JUST IN THE HUSH
before the dawn
A little wistful wind is born.
A little chilly errant breeze,
That thrills the grasses, stirs the trees.
And, as it wanders on its way,
While yet the night is cool and dark,
Ere the first carol of the lark,—
Its plaintive murmurs seem to say
" I wait the sorrows of the day."

TWO SONGS BY SITARA, OF KASHMIR

BELOVED !
your hair was golden
As tender tints of sunrise,
As corn beside the River
In softly varying hues.
I loved you for your slightness,
Your melancholy sweetness,
Your changeful eyes, that promised
What your lips would still refuse.

You came to me, and loved me,
Were mine upon the River,
The azure waters saw us
And the blue transparent sky;
The Lotus flowers knew it
Our happiness together,
While life was only River,
Only love, and you and I.

Love wakened on the River,
To sounds of running water,
With silver Stars for witness
And reflected Stars for light;
Awakened to existence,
With ripples for first music
And sunlight on the River
For earliest sense of sight.

Two Songs by Sitara, of Kashmir

Love grew upon the River
Among the scented flowers,
The open rosy flowers
Of the Lotus buds in bloom—
Love, brilliant as the Morning,
More fervent than the Noon-day,
And tender as the Twilight
In its blue transparent gloom.

Love died upon the River !
Cold snow upon the mountains,
The Lotus leaves turned yellow
And the water very grey.
Our kisses faint and falter,
The clinging hands unfasten,
The golden time is over
And our passion dies away.

Away. To be forgotten,
A ripple on the River,
That flashes in the sunset,
That flashed,—and died away.

SECOND SONG: THE GIRL FROM BALTISTAN

THROB, THROB, THROB,
Far away in the blue transparent Night,
On the outer horizon of dreaming
consciousness,
She hears the sound of her lover's
nearing boat
Afar, afloat,
On the river's loneliness,
where the Stars are the only light.
Hears the sound of the straining wood
Like a broken sob
Of a heart's distress,
Loving, misunderstood.

She lies, with her loose hair spent in soft disorder,
On a silken sheet with a purple woven border,
Every cell of her brain is latent fire,
Every fibre tense with restrained desire.
And the straining oars sound clearer, clearer,
The boat is approaching nearer, nearer,
" How to wait through the moments' space
Till I see the light of my lover's face ? "

Throb, throb, throb,
The sound dies down the stream
Till it only clings at the senses' edge
Like a half-remembered dream.

Doubtless, he in the silence lies,
His fair face turned to the tender skies,
Starlight touching his sleeping eyes.
While his boat is caught in the thickset sedge
And the waters round it gurgle and sob,
Or floats set free on the river's tide,
Oars laid aside.

She is awake and knows no rest,
Passion dies and is dispossessed
Of his brief, despotic power.
But the brain, once kindled, would still be afire
Were the whole world pasture to its desire,
And all of love, in a single hour,—
A single wine cup, filled to the brim,
Given to slake its thirst.

Some there are who are thus-wise cursed;
Times that follow fulfilled desire
Are of all their hours the worst,
They find no Respite and reach no Rest,
Though passion fail and desire grow dim,
No assuagement comes from the thing possessed
For possession feeds the fire.

" Oh, for the life of the bright hued things
Whose marriage and death are one,
A floating fusion on golden wings,
Alit with passion and sun ! "

Second
Song:
The Girl
from
Baltisan

" But we who re-marry a thousand times,
As the spirit or sense will,
In a thousand ways, in a thousand climes,
We remain unsatisfied still."

As her lover left her, alone, awake she lies,
With a sleepless brain and weary,
half-closed eyes
She turns her face where the purple silk
is spread,
Still sweet with delicate perfume
his presence shed
Her arms remember his vanished beauty still,
And, reminiscent of clustered curls,
her fingers thrill.
While the wonderful, Starlit Night
wears slowly on
Till the light of another day, serene and wan,
Pierces the eastern skies.

PALM TREES BY THE SEA

LOVE, LET ME THANK YOU FOR THIS !
Now we have drifted apart,
Wandered away from the Sea,—
For the fresh touch of your kiss,
For the young warmth of your heart,
For your youth given to me.

Thanks: for the curls of your hair,
Softer than silk to the hand,
For the clear gaze of your eyes.
For yourself: delicate, fair,
Seen as you lay on the sand,
Under the violet skies.

Thanks: for the words that you said,—
Secretly, tenderly sweet,
All through the tropical day,
Till, when the sunset was red,
I who lay still at your feet,
Felt my life ebbing away,

Weary and worn with desire,
Only yourself could console.
Love let me thank you for this !
For that fierce fervour and fire
Burnt through my lips to my soul
From the white heat of your kiss !

Palm
Trees by
the Sea

You were the essence of Spring,
Wayward and bright as a flame.
Though we have drifted apart,
Still how the syllables sing
Mixed in your musical name,
Deep in the well of my heart !

Once in the lingering light,
Thrown from the west on the Sea,
Laid you your garments aside,
Slender and goldenly bright,
Glimmered your beauty, set free,
Bright as a pearl in the tide.

Once, ere the thrill of the dawn
Silvered the edge of the sea,
I, who lay watching you rest,—
Pale in the chill of the morn,
Found you still dreaming of me,
Still by Love's fancies possessed.

Fallen on sorrowful days,
Love, let me thank you for this,
You were so happy with me !
Wrapped in Youth's roseate haze,
Wanting no more than my kiss
By the blue edge of the sea !

Ah, for those nights on the sand
Under the palms by the sea,
For the strange dream of those days
Spent in the passionate land,
For your youth given to me,
I am your debtor always !

SONG BY GULBAZ

"IS IT SAFE TO LIE SO LONELY WHEN THE SUMMER
twilight closes
No companion maidens, only you asleep among the roses ?

" Thirteen, fourteen years you number, and your hair is
soft and scented,
Perilous is such a slumber in the twilight all untented.

" Lonely loveliness means danger, lying in your rose-leaf nest,
What if some young passing stranger broke into your
careless rest ? "

But she would not heed the warning, lay alone serene
and slight,
Till the rosy spears of morning slew the darkness of the night.

Young love, walking softly, found her, in the scented,
shady closes
Threw his ardent arms around her, kissed her lips
beneath the roses.

And she said, with smiles and blushes, " Would that I had
sooner known !
Never now the morning thrushes wake and find me all alone.

" Since you said the roseleaf cover sweet protection gave,
but slight,
I have found this dear young lover to protect me through
the night ! "

KASHMIRI SONG

PALE HANDS I LOVED
beside the Shalimar,
Where are you now ?
Who lies beneath your spell !
Whom do you lead on Rapture's
roadway, far,
Before you agonise them in farewell ?

Oh, pale dispensers of my Joys and Pains,
Holding the doors of Heaven and of Hell,
How the hot blood rushed wildly
through the veins
Beneath your touch, until you waved farewell.

Pale hands, pink tipped,
lie Lotus buds that float
On those cool waters where we used to dwell,
I would have rather felt you round my throat
Crushing out life; than waving me farewell !

REVERIE OF ORMUZ THE PERSIAN

SOFTLY THE FEATHERY PALM-TREES FADE
in the violet Distance,
Faintly the lingering light touches the edge of the sea,
Sadly the Music of Waves, drifts, faint as an Anthem's
insistence,
Heard in the aisles of a dream, over the sandhills, to me.

Now that the Lights are reversed, and the Singing changed
into sighing,
Now that the wings of our fierce, fugitive passion are furled,
Take I unto myself, all alone in the light that is dying,
Much of the sorrow that lies hid at the Heart of the World.

Sad am I, sad for your loss: for failing the charm of your presence,
Even the sunshine has paled, leaving the Zenith less blue.
Even the ocean lessens the light of its green opalescence,
Since, to my sorrow I loved, loved and grew weary of, you.

Why was our passion so fleeting, why had the flush of
your beauty
Only so slender a spell, only so futile a power ?
Yet, even thus ever is life, save when long custom or duty
Moulds into sober fruit Love's fragile and fugitive flower.

Fain would my soul have been faithful; never an alien pleasure
Lured me away from the light lit in your luminous eyes,
But ever desire of the Mind, satisfied once, and at leisure
To criticise, balance, take counsel, assuredly dies.

Reverie of Ormuz the Persian

Three Songs of Zahir~U~Din

The Regret of the Ranee in the Hall of the Peacocks

Famine Song

Reverie of Ormuz the Persian

All through the centuries Man has gathered his flower,
    & fenced it,
—Infinite strife to attain; infinite struggle to keep,—
Holding his treasure awhile, all Fate and all forces
    against it,
Knowing it his no more, if ever his vigilance sleep.

But we have altered the World as pitiful man has
    grown stronger,
So that the things we love are as easily kept as won,
Therefore the ancient fight can engage and detain us no
longer,
And all to swiftly, alas, passion is over and done.

Far too speedily now we can gather the coveted treasure,
Enjoy it awhile, be satiated, begin to tire;
And what shall be done henceforth with the profitless
    after-leisure,
Who has the breath to kindle the ash of a faded fire ?

Ah, if it only had lasted ! After my ardent endeavour
Came the delirious Joy, flooding my life like a sea,
Days of delight that are burnt on the brain for ever and ever,
Days and nights when you loved, before you grew
    weary of me.

Softly the sunset decreases dim in the violet Distance,
Even as Love's own fervour has faded away from me,
Leaving the weariness, the monotonous
    Weight of Existence,—
All the farewells in the world weep in the sound of the sea.

SUNSTROKE

OH, STRAIGHT WHITE ROAD
that runs to meet,
Across green fields, the blue green sea,
You knew the little weary feet
Of my child bride that was to be !

Her people brought her from the shore
One golden day in sultry June,
And I stood, waiting, at the door,
Praying my eyes might see her soon.

With eager arms, wide open thrown,
Now never to be satisfied !
Ere I could make my love my own
She closed her amber eyes and died.

Alas ! alas ! they took no heed
How frail she was, my little one,
But brought her here with cruel speed
Beneath the fierce, relentless sun.

We laid her on the marriage bed
The bridle flowers in her hand,
A maiden from the ocean led
Only, alas ! to die inland.

I walk alone; the air is sweet,
The white road wanders to the sea,
I dream of those two little feet
That grew so tired in reaching me.

ADORATION

WHO DOES NOT FEEL
desire unending
To solace through his daily strife
With some mysterious
Mental blending,
The hungry loneliness of life ?

Until, by sudden passion shaken,
As terriers shake a rat at play,
He finds, all blindly, he has taken
The old, Hereditary way.

Yet, in the moment of communion,
The very heart of passion's fire,
His spirit spurns the mortal union,
" Not this, not this the Soul's desire ! "

Oh You, by whom my life is riven,
And reft away from my control.
Take back the hours of passion given !
Love me one moment from your soul.

Although I once, in ardent fashion,
Implored you long to give me this;
(In hopes to stem, or stifle, passion)
Your hair to touch, your lips to kiss.

Adoration

Now that your gracious self has granted
The loveliness you hold as naught,
I find, alas ! not that I wanted—
Possession has not stifled Thought.

Desire its aim has only shifted,—
Built hopes upon another plan,
And I in love for you have drifted
Beyond all passion known to man.

Beyond all dreams of soft caresses
The solacing of any kiss,—
Beyond the fragrance of your tresses
(Once I had sold my soul for this !)

But now I crave no mortal union
(Thanks for that sweetness in the past.)
I need some subtle, strange communion,
Some sense that I join you at last.

Long past the pulse and pain of passion,
Long left the limits of all love,—
I crave some nearer, fuller fashion,
Some unknown way, beyond, above,—

Some infinitely inner fusion,
As Wave with Water; Flame with Fire,—
Let me dream, once the dear delusion
That I am You, Oh, Heart's Desire !

Your kindness lent to my caresses
That beauty you so lightly prize,—
The midnight of your sable tresses,
The twilight of your shadowed eyes.

Ah, for that gift all thanks are given !
Yet, Oh, adored, beyond control,
Count all the passionate past forgiven
And love me once, once, from your soul !

THREE SONGS OF ZAHIR-U-DIN

THE TROPIC DAY'S
redundant charms
Cool twilight soothes away,
The sun slips down behind
the palms
And leaves the landscape grey.
I want to take you in my arms !
And kiss your lips away !

I wake with sunshine in my eyes
And find the morning blue,
A night of dreams behind me lies
And all were dreams of you !
Ah, how I wish the while I rise,
That what I dream were true.

The weary day's laborious pace,
I hasten and beguile
By fancies, which I backwards trace
To things I loved erstwhile;
The weary sweetness of your face,
Your faint, illusive smile.

The silken softness of your hair
Where faint bronze shadows are,
Your strangely slight and youthful air,
No passions seem to mar,—

Oh, why, since Fate has made you fair,
Must fortune keep you far ?

Thus spent, the day so long and bright
Less hot and brilliant seems,
Till in a final flare of light
The sun withdraws his beams.
Then, in the coolness of the night,
I meet you in my dreams !

SECOND SONG

HOW MUCH I LOVED
that way you had
Of smiling most, when very sad,
A smile which carried
tender hints
Of delicate tints
And warbling birds,
Of sun and spring,
And yet, more than all other thing,
Of Weariness beyond all Words !

None other ever smiled that way,
None that I know,—
The essence of all Gaiety lay
—Of all mad mirth that men may know,—
In that sad smile, serene and slow,
That on your lips was wont to play.

It needed many delicate lines
And subtle curves and roseate tints
To make that weary radiant smile;
It flickered, as beneath the vines
The sunshine through green shadow glints
On the pale path that lies below,
Flickered and flashed, and died away,
But the strange thoughts it woke meanwhile
Were wont to stay.

Second Song

Thoughts of Strange Things
you used to know
In dim, dead lives, lived long ago,
Some madly mirthful Merriment
Whose lingering light is yet unspent,—
Some unimaginable Woe,—
Your strange, sad smile forgets these not,
Though you, yourself, long since, forgot !

THIRD SONG, WRITTEN DURING FEVER

TO-NIGHT THE CLOUDS
hang very low,
They take the Hill-tops
to their breast,
And lay their arms about the fields.
The wind that fans me lying low,
Restless with great desire for rest,
No cooling touch of freshness yields.

I, sleepless through the stifling heat,
Watch the pale Lightning's constant glow
Between the wide set open doors.
I lie and long amidst the heat,—
The fever that my senses know,
For that cool slenderness of yours.

So delicate and cool you are !
A roseleaf that has lain in snow,
A snowflake tinged with sunset fire.
You do not know, so young you are,
How Fever fans the senses' glow
To uncontrollable desire !

And fills the spaces of the night
With furious and frantic thought,
One would not dare to think by day.

Ah, if you came to me to-night
These visions would be turned to naught,
These hateful dreams be held at bay !

But you are far, and Loneliness
My only lover through the night,
And not for any word or prayer
Would you console my loneliness
Or lend yourself, serene and slight,
And the cool clusters of your hair.

All through the night I long for you,
As shipwrecked men in tropics yearn
For the fresh fancies follow you
As dying men in deserts turn
Their thoughts to clear and chilly things.

Such dreams are mine, and such my thirst,
Unceasing and unsatisfied,
Until the night is burnt away
Among these dreams and fevered thirst,
And, through the open doorways, glide
The white feet of the coming day.

THE REGRET OF THE RANEE IN THE HALL OF PEACOCKS

THIS MAN HAS TAKEN
my Husband's life
And laid my Brethren low,
No sister indeed, were I, no wife,
To pardon and let him go.

Yet why does he look so young and slim
As he weak and wounded lies ?
How hard for me to be harsh to him,
With his soft, appealing eyes.

His hair is ruffled upon the stone
And the slender wrists are bound,
So young ! and yet he has overthrown
His scores on the battle ground.

Would I were only a slave to-day,
To whom it were right and meet
To wash the stains of the War away,
The dust from the weary feet.

Were I but one of my serving girls
To solace his pain to rest !
Shake out the sand from
the soft loose curls,
And hold him against my breast !

Have we such beauty about our Throne ?
Such lithe and delicate strength ?
Would God that I were the senseless stone
To support his slender length !

I hate those wounds that trouble my sight,
Unknown ! how I wish you lay,
Alone in my silken tent to-night
While I charmed the pain away !

I would lay you down on the Royal bed,
I would bathe your wounds with wine,
And setting your feet against my head
Dream you were lover of mine.

My Crown is heavy upon my hair,
The Jewels weigh on my breast,
All I would leave, with delight, to share
Your pale and passionate rest !

But hands grow restless about their swords,
Lips murmur below their breath,
" The Queen is silent too long ! "
" My Lords,
—Take him away to death ! "

PROTEST: BY ZAHIR-U-DIN

ALAS ! ALAS ! THIS WASTED NIGHT
With all its Jamin-scented air,
Its thousand stars, serenely bright !
I lie alone, and long for you,
Long for your Champa-scented hair,
Your tranquil eyes of twilight hue.

Long for the close-curved, delicate lips
—Their sinuous sweetness laid on mine—
Here, where the slender fountain drips,
Here, where the yellow roses glow,
Pale in the tender silver shine
The stars across the garden throw.

Alas ! alas ! poor passionate Youth !
Why must he spend these lonely nights ?
The poets hardly speak the truth,—
Despite their praiseful litany,
His season is not all delights
Nor every night an ecstasy !

The very power and passion that make,
Might make,—his days one golden dream,
How he must suffer for their sake !
Till, in their fierce and futile rage,
The baffled senses almost deem
They might be happier in old age.

Age that can find red roses sweet,
And yet not crave a rose-red mouth;
Hear Bulbuls, with no wish that feet
Of sweeter singers went his way:
Inhale warm breezes from the South,
Yet never feel his fancy stray.

Protest: By Zahir-u-Din

From some near Village I can hear
The cadenced throbbing of a drum,
Now softly distant, now more near;
And in an almost human fashion,
It, plaintive, wistful, seems to come
Laden with sighs of fitful passion.

To mock me, lying here alone
Among the thousand useless flowers
Upon the fountain's border stone.
Cold stone, that chills me as I lie
Counting the slowly passing hours
By the white spangles in the sky.

Some feast the Tom-toms celebrate,
Where close together, side by side,
Gay in their gauze and tinsel state
With lips serene and downcast eyes,
Sit the young bridegroom and his bride,
While round them songs and laughter rise.

They are together; Why are we
So hopelessly, so far apart ?

Protest: By Zahir-u-Din

Oh, I implore you, come to me !
Come to me, Solace of mine eyes !
Come Consolation of my heart !
Light of my senses ! What replies ?

A little, languid, mocking breeze
That rustles through the Jasmin flowers
And stirs among the Tamarind trees.
A little gurgle of the spray
That drips, unheard, through silent hours.
Then breaks in sudden bubbling play.

Wind, have you never loved a rose ?
And water, seek you not the Sea ?
Why, therefore, mock at my repose ?
It is my fault I am alone
Beneath the feathery Tamarind tree
Whose shadows over me are thrown ?

Nay, I am mad indeed, with thirst
For all to me this night denied
And drunk with longing, and accurst
Beyond all chance of sleep or rest,
With love, unslaked, unsatisfied,
And dreams of beauty unpossessed.

Hating the hour that brings you not,
Mad at the space betwixt us twain,
Sad for my empty arms, so hot
And fevered, even the chilly stone
Can scarcely cool their burning pain,—
And oh, this sense of being alone !

Protest: By Zahir-u-Din

Take hence, Oh, Night, your wasted hours,
You bring me not my Life's Delight,
My Star of Stars, my flower of Flowers !
You leave me loveless and forlorn,
Pass on, most false and futile night,
Pass on and perish in the Dawn !

FAMINE SONG

DEATH AND FAMINE ON
every side
And never a sign of rain,
The bones of those who have
starved and died
Unburied upon the plain.
What care have I that the bones bleach white ?
To-morrow they may be mine,
But I shall sleep in your arms to-night
And drink your lips like wine !

Cholera, Riot and Sudden Death
And the brave red blood set free,
The glazing eye and the failing breath,—
But what are these things to me ?
Your breath is quick and your eyes are bright
And your blood is red like wine,
And I shall sleep in your arms to-night
And hold your lips with mine !

I hear the sound of a thousand tears,
Like softly pattering rain,
I see the fever, folly and fears
Fulfilling man's tale of pain.
But for the moment your star is bright,
I revel beneath its shine,
For I shall sleep in your arms to-night
And feel your lips on mine !

And you need not deem me over cold,
That I do not stop to think
For all the pleasure this Life may hold
Is on the Precipice brink.
Thought could but lessen my soul's delight,
And to-day she may not pine.
For I shall lie in your arms to-night
And close your lips with mine !

I trust what sorrow the Fates may send
I may carry quietly through,
And pray for grace when I reach the end,
To die as a man should do.
To-day, at least, must be clear and bright,
Without a sorrowful sign,
Because I sleep in your arms to-night
And feel your lips on mine !

So on I work, in the blazing sun,
To bury what dead we may,
But glad, oh, glad, when the day is done
And the night falls round us grey.
Would those we covered away from sight
Had a rest so sweet as mine !
For I shall sleep in your arms to-night
And drink your lips like wine !

THE WINDOW OVER-LOOKING THE HARBOUR

SAD IS THE EVENING:
all the level sand
Lies left and lonely, while the restless sea,
Tired of the green caresses of the land,
Withdraws into its own infinity.

But still more sad this white and chilly Dawn
Filling the vacant spaces of the sky,
While little winds blow here and there forlorn
And all the stars, weary of shining, die.

And more than desolate, to wake, to rise,
Leaving the couch, where softly sleeping still,
What through the past night made my heaven, lies;
And looking out across the window sill

See, from the upper window's vantage ground,
Mankind slip into harness once again,
And wearily resume his daily round
Of love and labour, toil and strife and pain.

How the sad thoughts slip back across the night:
The whole thing seems so aimless and so vain.
What use the raptures, passion and delight,
Burnt out; as though they could not wake again.

The worn-out nerves and weary brain repeat
The question: Whither all these passions tend;—
This curious thirst, so painful and so sweet,
So fierce, so very short-lived, to what end ?

Even, if seeking for ourselves, the Race,
The only immortality we know,—
Even if from the flower of our embrace
Some spark should kindle, or some fruit should grow,

What were the use ? the gain, to us or it,
That we should cause another You or I,—
Another life, from our light passion lit,
To suffer like ourselves awhile and die.

What aim, what end indeed ? Our being runs
In a closed circle. All we know or see
Tends to assure us that a thousand suns,
Teeming perchance with life, have ceased to be.

Ah, the grey Dawn seems more than desolate,
And the past night of passion worse than waste,
Love but a useless flower, that soon or late,
Turns to a fruit with bitter aftertaste.

Youth, even Youth, seems futile and forlorn
While the new day grows slowly white above.
Pale and reproachful comes the chilly Dawn
After the fervour of a night of love.

BACK TO THE BORDER

THE TREMULOUS MORNING
is breaking
Against the white waste of the sky,
And hundreds of birds are awaking
In tamarisk bushes hard by.
I, waiting alone in the station,
Can hear in the distance, grey-blue,
The sound of that iron desolation,
The train that will bear me from you.

'Twill carry me under your casement,
You'll feel in your dreams as you lie
The quiver, from gable to basement,
The rush of my train sweeping by.
And I shall look out as I pass it,—
Your dear, unforgettable door,
'Twas ours till last night, but alas ! it
Will never be mine any more.

Through twilight blue-grey and uncertain,
Where frost leaves the window-pane free
I'll look at the tinsel-edged curtain
That hid so much pleasure for me.
I go to my long undone duty
Alone in the chill and the gloom,
My eyes are still full of the beauty
I leave in your rose-scented room.

Lie still in your dreams; for your tresses
Are free of my lingering kiss.
I keep you awake with caresses
No longer; be happy in this !
From passion you told me you hated
You're now and for ever set free,
I pass in my train sorrow weighted,
Your house that was Heaven to me.

You won't find a trace, when you waken,
Of me or my love of the past,
Rise up and rejoice ! I have taken
My longed-for departure at last.
My fervent and useless persistence
You never need suffer again,
Nor even perceive in the distance
The smoke of my vanishing train !

REVERIE: ZAHIR-U-DIN

ALONE, I WAIT, TILL HER TWILIGHT GATE
The Night slips quietly through
With shadow and gloom, and purple bloom,
Flung over the Zenith blue.

Her stars that tremble, would fain dissemble
Light over lovers thrown,—
Her hush and mystery knows no history
Such as day may own.
Day has record of pleasure and pain,
But things that are done by Night remain
For ever and ever unknown.

For a thousand years, 'neath a thousand skies,
Night has brought men love;
Therefore the old, old longings rise
As the light grows dim above.

Therefore, now that the shadows close,
And the mists rise weird and white,
While Time is scented with musk and rose;
Magic with silver light.

I long for love; will you grant me some ?
Day is over at last.
Come ! as lovers have always come,
Through the evenings of the Past.
Swiftly, as lovers have always come,
Softly, as lovers have always come
Through the long-forgotten Past.

SEA SONG

AGAINST THE PLANKS OF THE CABIN SIDE,
(So slight a thing between them and me,)
The great waves thundered and throbbed
and sighed,
The great green waves of the Indian sea !

Your face was white as the foam is white,
Your hair was curled as the waves are curled,
I would we had steamed and reached that night
The sea's last edge, the end of the world.

The wind blew in through the open port,
So freshly joyous and salt and free,
Your hair it lifted, your lips it sought,
And then swept back to the open sea.

The engines throbbed with their constant beat;
Your heart was nearer, and all I heard,
Your lips were salt, but I found them sweet,
While, acquiescent, you spoke no word.

So straight you lay in your narrow berth,
Rocked by the waves; and you seemed to be
Essence of all that is sweet on earth,
Of all that is sad and strange at sea.

And you were white as the foam is white,
Your hair was curled as the waves are curled.
Ah ! had we but sailed and reached that night,
The sea's last edge, the end of the world !

TO THE HILLS !

'TIS EIGHT MILES OUT,
and eight miles in,
Just at the break of morn.
'Tis ice without and flame within,
To gain a kiss at dawn !

Far, where the Lilac Hills arise
Soft from the misty plain,
A lone, enchanted hollow lies
Where I at last draw rein.

Midwinter grips this lonely land,
This stony, treeless waste,
Where East, due East, across the sand,
We fly in fevered haste.

Pull up ! the East will soon be red,
The wild duck westward fly,
And make above my anxious head,
Triangles in the sky.

Like wind we go; we both are still
So young; all thanks to Fate !
(It cuts like knives, this air so chill,)
Dear God ! if I am late !

Behind us, wrapped in mist and sleep
The Ruined City lies,
(Although we race, we seem to creep !)
While lighter grow the skies.

To the Hills !

Eight miles out only, eight miles in,
Good going all the way;
But more and more the clouds begin
To redden into day.

And every snow-tipped peak grows pink
An iridescent gem !
My heart beats quick, with joy, to think
How I am nearing them !

As mile on mile behind us falls,
Till, Oh, delight ! I see,
My Heart's Desire, who softly calls
Across the gloom to me.

The utter joy of that First Love
No later love has given,
When, while the skies grew light above,
We entered into Heaven.

TILL I WAKE

WHEN I AM DYING,
lean over me tenderly, softly,
Stoop, as the yellow roses droop
in the wind from the South,
So I may when I wake,
if there be an Awakening,
Keep, what lulled me to sleep,
the touch of your lips on my mouth.

HIS RUBIES: TOLD BY VALGOVIND

ALONG THE HOT
and endless road
Calm and erect, with haggard eyes,
The prisoner bore his fetters' load
Beneath the scorching, azure skies.

Serene and tall, with brows unbent,
Without a hope, without a friend,
He, under escort, onward went,
With death to meet him at the end.

The Poppy fields were pink and gay
On either side, and in the heat
Their drowsy scent exhaled all day
A dream-like fragrance almost sweet.

And when the cool of evening fell
And tender colours touched the sky,
He still felt youth within him dwell
And half forgot he had to die.

Sometimes at night, the Camp-fires lit
And casting fitful light around,
His guard would, friend-like, let him sit
And talk awhile with them, unbound.

Thus they, the night before the last,
Were resting, when a group of girls

Across the small encampment passed,
With laughing lips and scented curls.

Then in the Prisoner's weary eyes
A sudden light lit up once more,
The women saw him with surprise,
And pity for the chains he bore.

For little women reck of Crime
If young and fair the criminal be
Here in this tropic, amorous clime
Where love is still untamed and free.

And one there was, she walked less fast
Behind the rest, perhaps beguiled
By his lithe form, who as she passed,
Waited a little while, and smiled.

The guard, in kindly Eastern fashion,
Smiled to themselves, and let her stay
So tolerant of human passion,
" To love he has but one more day."

Yet when (the soft and scented gloom
Scarce lighted by the dying fire)
His arms caressed her youth and bloom,
With him it was not all desire.

" For me," he whispered, as he lay,
" But little life remains to live.

One thing I crave to take away:
You have the gift; but will you give ?

" If I could know some child of mine
Would live his life, and see the sun
Across these fields of poppies shine,
What should I care that mine is done ?

" To die would not be dying quite,
Leaving a little life behind,
You, were you kind to me to-night,
Could grant me this; but—are you kind ?

" See, I have something here for you,
For you and It, if It there be."
Soft in the gloom her glances grew,
With gentle tears he could not see.

He took the chain from off his neck.
Hid in the silver charm there lay
Three rubies, without flaw or fleck.
She answered softly, " I will stay."

He drew her close; the moonless skies
Shed little light; the fire was dead.
Soft pity filled her youthful eyes,
And many tender things she said.

Throughout the hot and silent night
All that he asked of her she gave.

And, left alone ere morning light,
He went serenely to the grave,

Happy; for even when the rope
Confined his neck, his thoughts were free,
And centred round his Secret Hope
The little life that was to be.

When Poppies bloomed again, she bore
His child who gaily laughed and crowed,
While round his tiny neck he wore
The rubies given on the road.

For his small sake she wished to wait,
But vainly to forget she tried,
And grieving for the Prisoner's fate,
She broke her gentle heart and died.

Lalila to the Ferengi Lover

There is no Breeze to Cool the Heat of Love

The Temple Dancing Girl

Song of the Devoted Slave

SONG OF TAJ MAHOMED

DEAR IS MY INLAID SWORD;
across the Border
It brought me much reward;
dear is my Mistress,
The jewelled treasure of an amorous hour
Dear beyond measure are my dreams and Fancies.

These I adore; for these I live and labour,
Holding them more than sword
or jewelled Mistress,
For this indeed my rust, and that prove faithless,
But, till my limbs are dust, I have my Fancies.

THE GARDEN OF KAMA; KAMA THE INDIAN EROS

THE DAYLIGHT IS DYING,
The flying fox flying,
Amber and amethyst burn in the sky.
See, the sun throws a late,
Lingering, roseate
Kiss to the landscape to bid it good-bye.

The time of our Trysting !
Oh, come, unresisting,
Lovely, expectant, on tentative feet.
Shadow shall cover us,
Roses bend over us,
Making a bride chamber sacred and sweet.

We know not Life's reason,
The length of its season,
Know not if they know, the great Ones above.
We none of us sought it,
And few could support it,
Were it not gilt with the glamour of love.

But much is forgiven,
To Gods who have given,
If but for an hour the Rapture of Youth.

You do not yet know it,
But Kama shall show it,
Changing your dreams to his Exquisite Truth.

The Fireflies shall light you,
And naught shall affright you,
Nothing shall trouble the Flight of the Hours.
Come, for I wait for you,
Night is too late for you,
Come, when the twilight is closing the flowers.

Every breeze still is,
And, scented with lilies,
Cooled by the twilight, refreshed by the dew,
The garden lies breathless,
Where Kama, the Deathless,
In the hushed starlight, is waiting for you.

CAMP FOLLOWER'S SONG, GOMAL RIVER

WE HAVE LEFT GUL KACH
behind us,
Are marching on Apozai,—
Where pleasure and rest are waiting
To welcome us by and by.

We're falling back from the Gomal.
Across the Gir-dao plain,
The camping ground is deserted,
We'll never come back again.

Along the rocks and the defiles,
The mules and the camels wind.
Good-bye to Rahimut-Ullah,
The man who is left behind.

For some we lost in the skirmish,
And some were killed in the fight.
But he was captured by fever,
In the sentry pit, at night.

A rifle shot had been swifter,
Less trouble a sabre thrust,
But his Fate decided fever,
And each man dies as he must.

Behind us, red in the distance,
The wavering flames rise high,

The flames of our burning grass-huts,
Against the black of the sky.

We hear the sound of the river,
And ever-lessening moan,
The hearts of us all turn backwards
To where he is left alone.

We sing up a little louder,
We know that we feel bereft,
We're leaving the camp together,
And only one of us left.

The only one, out of many,
And each must come to his end,
I wish I could stop this singing,
He happened to be my friend.

We're falling back from the Gomal.
We're marching on Apozai,
And pleasure and rest are waiting
To welcome us by and by.

Perhaps the feast will taste bitter,
The lips of the girls less kind,—
Because of Rahimut-Ullah,
The man who is left behind.

Camp Follower's Song, Gomal River

SONG OF THE COLOURS: BY TAJ MAHOMED

ROSECOLOUR

ROSE PINK AM I, THE COLOUR
gleams and glows
In many a flower; her lips,
those tender doors
By which, in time of love,
love's essence flows
From him to her, are dyed in delicate Rose.
Mine is the earliest Ruby light that pours
Out of the East, when day's white gates unclose.

On downy peach, and maiden's downier cheek
I, in a flush of radiant bloom, alight,
Clinging, at sunset, to the shimmering peak
I veil its snow in floods of Roseate light.

AZURE

Mine is the heavenly hue of Azure skies,
Where the white clouds lie softly as seraph's wings,
Mine the sweet, shadowed light in innocent eyes,
Whose lovely looks light only on lovely things.

Mine the Blue Distance, delicate and clear.
Mine the Blue Glory of the morning sea,
All that the soul so longs for, finds not here,
Fond eyes deceive themselves, and find in me.

SCARLET

Hail ! to the Royal Red of living Blood,
Let loose by steel in spirit freeing flood,
Forced from faint forms, by toil or torture torn
Staining the patient gates of life new born.

Colour of War and Rage, of Pomp and Show,
Banners that flash, red flags that flaunt and glow,
Colour of Carnage, Glory, also Shame,
Raiment of those whom women may not name.

I hid in mines, where unborn Rubies dwell,
Flicker and flare in fitful fire in Hell,
The outpressed life-blood of the grape is mine,
Hail ! to the Royal Purple Red of Wine.

Strong am I, over strong, to eyes that tire,
In the hot hue of Rapine, Riot, Flame,
Death and Despair are black, War and Desire,
The two red cards in Life's unequal game.

GREEN

I am the Life of Forests, and Wandering Streams,
Green as the feathery reeds the Florican love,
Young as a maiden who of her marriage dreams,
Still sweetly inexperienced in ways of Love.

Colour of Youth and Hope, some waves are mine,
Some emerald reaches of the evening sky.

See, in the Spring, my sweet green
Promise shine,
Never to be fulfilled, of by and by.

Never to be fulfilled; leaves bud and ever
Something is wanting, something falls behind,
The flowered Solstice comes indeed, but never
That light and lovely summer men divined.

VIOLET

I were the colour of Things (if hue they had)
That are hard to name.
Of curious, twisted thoughts
that men call " mad "
Or oftener " shame."
Of that delicate vice, that is hardly vice,
So reticent, rare,
Ethereal, as the scent of buds and spice,
In this Eastern air.

On palm fringed shores I colour
the Cowrie shell
With its edges curled.
And deep in Datura poison buds I dwell
In a perfumed world.
My lilac tinges the edge of the evening sky
Where the sunset clings.
My purple lends an Imperial Majesty
To the robes of kings.

YELLOW

Gold am I, and for me, ever men curse and pray,
Selling their souls and each other, by night and day.
A sordid colour, and yet, I make some things fair,
Dying sunsets, fields of corn, and a maiden's hair.

Thus they discoursed in the daytime,
        Violet, Yellow and Blue,
Emerald, Scarlet, and Rose colour,
        the pink and perfect hue.
Thus they spoke in the sunshine,
        when their beauty was manifest,
Till the Night came, and the Silence,
        and gave them an equal rest.

LALILA, TO THE FERENGI LOVER

WHY ABOVE OTHERS WAS
I so blessed
And honoured ? to be the chosen one
To hold you, sleeping, against my breast,
As now I may hold your only son.

Twelve months ago; that wonderful night !
You gave your life to me in a kiss,
Have I done well, for that past delight,
In return, to have given you this ?

Look down at his face, your face, beloved,
His eyes are azure as yours are blue.
In every line of his form is proved
How well I loved you, and only you.

I felt the secret hope at my heart
Turn suddenly to the living joy,
And knew that your life in mine had part
As golden grains in a brass alloy.

And learning thus, that your child was mine,
Thrilled by the sense of its stirring life,
I held myself as a sacred shrine
Afar from pleasure, and pain, and strife,

That all unworthy I might not be
Of that you had deigned to cause to dwell
Hidden away in the heart of me,
As white pearls hide in a dusky shell.

Do you remember, when first you laid
Your lips on mine, that enchanted night ?
My eyes were timid, my lips afraid,
You seemed so slender and strangely white.

I always trembled; the moments flew
Swiftly to dawn that took you away,
But this is a small and lovely you
Content to rest in my arms all day.

Oh, since you have sought me, Lord, for this,
And given your only child to me,
My life devoted to yours and his
Whilst I am living will always be.

And after death, through the long To Be.
(Which, I think, must surely keep love's laws,)
I, should you chance to have need of me,
Am ever and always, only yours.

ON THE CITY WALL

UPON THE CITY RAMPARTS,
lit up by sunset gleam,
The Blue eyes that conquer, meet the Darker eyes
that dream.

The Dark eyes, so Eastern,
and the Blue eyes from the West,
The last alight with action, the first so full of rest.

Brown, that seem to hold the Past; its magic mystery,
Blue, that catch the early light, of ages yet to be.

Meet and fall and meet again, then linger, look, and smile,
Time and distance all forgotten, for a little while.

Happy on the city wall, in the warm spring weather,
All the force of Nature's laws, drawing them together.

East and West so gaily blending, for a little space,
All the sunshine seems to centre, round th' Enchanted place !

One rides down the dusty road, one watches from the wall,
Azure eyes would fain return, and Amber eyes recall;

Would fain be on the ramparts, and resting heart to heart,
But time o' love is overpast, East and West must part.

Blue eyes so clear and brilliant ! Brown eyes so dark and deep !
Those are dim, and ride away, these cry themselves to sleep.

" Oh, since Love is all so short, the sob so near the smile,
Blue eyes that always conquer us, is it worth your while ? "

" LOVE LIGHTLY "

THERE WERE ROSES IN THE HEDGES,
and Sunshine in the sky,
Red Lilies in the sedges,
where the water rippled by,
A thousand Bulbuls singing,
oh, how jubilant they were,
And a thousand flowers flinging their sweetness on the air.

But you, who sat beside me, had a shadow in your eyes,
Their sadness seemed to chide me, when I gave you
scant replies;
You asked " Did I remember ? " and
" When had I ceased to care ? "
In vain you fanned the ember, for the love flame
was not there.

" And so, since you are tired of me, you ask me to forget,
What is the use of caring, now that you no longer care ?
When Love is dead, his Memory can only bring regret,
But how can I forget you with the flowers in your hair ? "

What use the scented Roses, or the azure of the sky ?
They are sweet when Love reposes, but then he had to die.
What could I do in leaving you, but ask you to forget,
I suffered too, in grieving you, I all but loved you yet.

But half love is treason, that no Lover can forgive,
I had loved you for a season, I had no more to give.

"Love Lightly"

You saw my passion faltered, for I could but let you see,
And it was not I that altered, but Fate that altered me.

And so, since I am tired of love, I ask you to forget,
What is the use you caring, now that I no longer care ?
When Love is dead, his Memory can only bring regret,
Forget me, oh, forget me, and my flower-scented hair !

NO RIVAL LIKE THE PAST

AS THOSE WHO EAT A LUSCIOUS FRUIT,
sunbaked,
Full of sweet juice, with zest, until they find
It finished, and their appetite unslaked,
And so return and eat the pared-off rind;—

We, who in Youth, set white and careless teeth
In the Ripe Fruits of Pleasure while they last,
Later, creep back to gnaw the cast-off sheath,
And find there is no Rival like the Past.

VERSE BY TAJ MAHOMED

WHEN FIRST I LOVED,
I gave my very soul
Utterly unreserved to Love's control,
But Love deceived me,
wrenched my youth away
And made the gold of lie for ever grey.
Long I lived lonely, yet I tried in vain
With any other Joy to stifle pain,
There is no other joy, I learned to know,
And so returned to Love, as long ago.
Yet I, this little while ere I go hence,
Love very lightly now, in self-defence.

LINES BY TAJ MAHOMED

THIS PASSION IS
but an ember
Of a Sun, of a Fire, long set,
I could not live and remember,
And so I love and forget.

You say, and the tone is fretful,
That my mourning days were few,
You call me over forgetful—
My God, if you only knew !

THERE IS NO BREEZE TO COOL THE HEAT OF LOVE

THE LISTLESS PALM-TREES
catch the breeze above
The pile-built huts that edge the salt Lagoon,
There is no Breeze to cool the heat of love,
No wind from land or sea, at night or noon.

Perfumed and robed I wait, my Lord, for you,
And my heart waits alert, with strained delight,
My flowers are loath to close, as though they knew
That you will come to me before the night.

In the Verandah all the lights are lit,
And softly veiled in rose to please your eyes,
Between the pillars flying foxes flit,
Their wings transparent on the lilac skies.

Come soon, my Lord, come soon, I almost fear
My heart may fail me in this keen suspense,
Break with delight, at last, to know you near.
Pleasure is one with Pain, if too intense.

I envy these; the steps that you will tread,
The jasmin that will touch you by its leaves,
When, in your slender height, you stoop your head
At the low door beneath the palm-thatched eaves.

For though you utterly belong to me,
And love has done his utmost 'twixt us twain,

There is no Breeze to Cool the Heat of Love

Your slightest, careless touch yet seems to be
That keen delight so much akin to pain.

The night breeze blows across the still Lagoon,
And stirs the Palm-trees till they wave above
Our pile-built huts; Oh, come my Lord, come soon,
There is no Breeze to cool the heat of love.

Every time you give yourself to me,
The gift seems greater, and yourself more fair,
This slight-built, palm-thatched hut has come to be
A temple, since, my Lord, you visit there.

And as the water, gurgling softly, goes
Among the piles beneath the slender floor;
I hear it murmur, as it seaward flows,
Of the great Wonder seen upon the shore.

The Miracle, that you should come to me,
Whom the whole world seeing, can but desire,
It is as though some White Star stooped to be
The messmate of our little cooking fire.

Leaving the Glory of his Purple Skies,
And the White Friendship of the Crescent Moon,
And yet;—I look into your brilliant eyes,
And find content; Oh, come, my Lord, come soon.

Perfumed and robed I wait for you, I wait,
The flowers that please you wreathed about my hair,
And this poor face set forth in jewelled state
So more than proud since you have found it fair.

There is no Breeze to Cool the Heat of Love

My lute is ready, and the fragrant drink
Your lips may honour, how it will rejoice
Losing its life in yours ! the lute I think
But wastes the time when I might hear your voice.

But you desired it; therefore I obey
Your slightest, as your utmost, wish or will,
Whether it please you to caress or slay
It would please me, to give obedience still.

I would delight to die beneath your kiss;
I envy that young maiden who was slain,
So her warm blood, flowing beneath the kriss,
Might ease the wounded Sultan of his pain.

If she loved him as I love you, my Lord;
There is no pleasure on the earth so sweet
As is the pain endured for one adored;
If I lay crushed beneath your slender feet.

I should be happy ! Ah, come soon, come soon,
See how the stars grow large and white above,
The land breeze blows across the salt Lagoon,
There is no Breeze to cool the heat of love.

MALAY SONG

THE STARS AWAIT,
serene and white,
The unarisen moon;
Oh, come and stay with me
to-night,
Beside the salt Lagoon !

My hut is small, but as you lie,
You see the lighted shore,
And hear the rippling water sigh
Beneath the pile-raised floor.

No gift have I of jewels or flowers,
My room is poor and bare:
But all the silver sea is ours,
And all the scented air.

Blown from the mainland;
where there grows
Th' " Intriguer of the Night,"
The flower that you have named
Tuberose,
Sweet scented, slim, and white.

The flower that when the air is still,
And no land breezes blow,
From its pale petals can distil
A phosphorescent glow.

Malay Song

I see your ship at anchor ride;
Her " captive lightning " shine.
Before she takes to-morrow's tide,
Let this one night be mine !

Though in the language of your land
My words are poor and few,
Oh, read my eyes, and understand,
I give my youth to you !

THE TEMPLE DANCING GIRL

YOU WILL BE MINE;
those lightly dancing feet,
Falling as softly on the careless street
As the wind-loosened petals of a flower,
Will bring you here, at the Appointed Hour.

And all the Temple's little links and laws
Will not for long protect your loveliness.
I have a stronger force to aid my cause,
Nature's great Law, to love and to possess !

Throughout those sleepless watches, when I lay
Wakeful, desiring what I might not see,
I knew, (it helped those hours, from dusk to day,)
In this one thing, Fate would be kind to me.

You will consent, through all my veins like wine
This prescience flows; your lips meet mine above,
Your clear soft eyes look upward into mine
Dim in a silent ecstasy of love.

The clustered softness of your waving hair,
That curious paleness which enchants me so,
And all your delicate strength and youthful air,
Destiny will compel you to bestow !

Refuse, withdraw and hesitate awhile
Your young reluctance does but fan the flame,

The Temple Dancing Girl

My partner, Love, waits, with a tender smile,
Who play against him play a loosing game.

I, strong in nothing else, have strength in this,
The subtlest, most resistless, force we know
Is aiding me; and you must stoop and kiss,
The genius of the race will have it so !

Yet, make it not too long, not too intense
My thirst: lest I should break beneath the strain.
And the worn nerves, and over-wearied sense,
Enjoy not what they spent themselves to gain.

Lest, in the hour when you consent to share
That human passion Beauty makes divine
I, over worn, should find you over fair,
Lest I should die before I make you mine.

You will consent, those slim, reluctant feet,
Falling as lightly on the careless street
As the white petals of a wind-worn flower,
Will bring you here, at the Appointed Hour.

HIRA-SINGH'S FAREWELL TO BURMAH

ON THE WOODEN DECK
of the wooden Junk, silent, alone, we lie,
With silver foam about the bow,
and a silver moon in the sky:
A glimmer of dimmer silver here,
from the anklets round your feet,
Our lips may close on each other's lips,
but never our souls may meet.

For though in my arms you lie at rest,
your name I have never heard,
To carry a thought between us two,
we have not a single word.
And yet what matter we do not speak,
when the ardent eyes have spoken,
The way of love is a sweeter way,
when the silence is unbroken.

As a wayward Fancy, tired at times,
of the cultured Damask Rose,
Drifts away to the tangled copse,
where the wild Anemone grows;
So the ordered and licit love ashore,
is hardly fresh and free
As this light love in the open wind
and salt of the outer sea.

So sweet you are, with your tinted cheeks
and your small caressive hands,
What if I carried you home with me,
where our Golden Temple Stands ?

Yet, this were folly indeed; to bind,
in fetters of permanence,
A passing dream whose enchantment charms
because of its transience.

Life is ever a slave to Time;
we have but an hour to rest,
Her steam is up and her lighters leave,
the vessel that takes me west;
And never again we two shall meet,
as we chance to meet to-night,
On the Junk, whose painted eyes gaze forth,
in desolate want of sight.

And what is love at its best, but this ?
conceived by a passing glance,
Nursed and reared in a transient mood,
on a drifting Sea of chance.
For rudderless craft are all our loves,
among the rocks and the shoals,
Well we may know one another's speech,
but never each other's souls.

Give here your lips and kiss me again,
we have but a moment more,
Before we set the sail to the mast,
before we loosen the oar.
Good-bye to you, and my thanks to you,
for the rest you let me share,
While this night drifted away to the Past,
to join the Nights that Were.

STARLIGHT

OH, BEAUTIFUL STARS,
when you see me go
Hither and thither, in search of love,
Do you think me faithless,
who gleam and glow
Serene and fixed in the blue above ?
Oh, Stars, so golden, it is not so.

But there is a garden I dare not see,
There is a place where I fear to go,
Since the charm and glory of life to me
The brown earth covered there, long ago.
Oh, Stars, you saw it, you know, you know.

Hither and thither I wandering go,
With aimless haste and weary fret;
In a search for pleasure and love ? Not so,
Seeking desperately to forget.
You see so many, Oh, Stars, you know.

SAMPAN SONG

A LITTLE BREEZE BLEW
over the sea,
And it came from far away,
Across the fields of millet and rice,
All warm with sunshine
and sweet with spice,
It lifted his curls and kissed him thrice,
As upon the deck he lay.

It said, " Oh, idle upon the sea,
Awake and with sleep have done,
Haul up the widest sail of the prow,
And come with me to the rice fields now,
She longs, oh, how can I tell you how,
To show you your first-born son ! "

SONG OF THE DEVOTED SLAVE

THERE IS ONE GOD:
MAHOMED HIS PROPHET.
Had I his power
I would take the topmost peaks
of the snow-clad Himalayas,
And range them around your dwelling,
during the heats of summer,
To cool the airs that fan your serene
and delicate presence,
Had I the power.

Your courtyard should ever be filled with the fleetest of camels
Laden with inlaid armour, jewels and trappings for horses,
Ripe dates from Egypt, and spices and musk from Arabia.
And the sacred waters of Zem-Zem well; transported thither,
Should bubble and flow in your chamber, to bathe the delicate
Slender and wayworn feet of my Lord, returning from travel,
Had I the power.

Fine woven silk, from the further East,
should conceal your beauty,
Clinging around you in amorous folds; caressive, silken,
Beautiful, long-lashed, sweet-voiced Persian boys should,
kneeling, serve you,
And the floor beneath your sandalled feet
should be smooth and golden,
Had I the power.

And if ever your clear and stately thoughts
should turn to women,
Kings' daughters, maidens, should be appointed
to your caresses,
That the youth and the strength of my Lord
might never be wasted
In light or sterile love; but enrich the world
with his children.

Whilst I should sit in the outer court
of the Water Palace
To await the time when you went forth,
for Pleasure or Warfare,
Descending the stairs rose crowned,
or armed and arrayed in purple,—
To mark the place where your steps had fallen,
and kiss the footprints,
Had I the power.

THE SINGER

THE SINGER ONLY SANG THE JOY OF LIFE,
For all to well, alas ! the singer knew
How hard the daily toil, how keen the strife,
How salt the falling tear; the joys how few.

He who thinks hard soon finds it hard to live,
Learning the Secret Bitterness of Things:
So, leaving thought, the singer strove to give
A level lightness to his lyric strings.

He only sang of Love; its joy and pain,
But each man in his early season loves;
Each finds the old, lost Paradise again,
Unfolding leaves, and roses, nesting doves.

And though that sunlit time flies all too fleetly,
Delightful Days that dance away too soon !
Its early morning freshness lingers sweetly
Throughout life's grey and tedious afternoon.

And he, whose dreams enshrine her tender eyes,
And she, whose senses wait his waking hand,
Impatient youth, that tired but sleepless lies,
Will read perhaps, and reading, understand.

Oh, roseate lips he would have loved to kiss,
Oh, eager lovers that he never knew !
What should you know of him, or words of his,
But all the songs he sang were sung for you !

FANCY

FAR IN THE FURTHER EAST
the skilful craftsman
Fashioned this fancy for the West's delight.
This rose and azure Dragon, crouching softly
Upon the satin skin, close-grained and white.

And you lay silent, while his slender needles
Pricked the intricate pattern on your arm,
Combining deftly Cruelty and Beauty,
That subtle union, whose child is charm.

Charm irresistible; the lovely something
We follow in our dreams, but may not reach,
The unattainable Divine Enchantment,
Hinted in music, never heard in speech.

This from the blue design exhales towards me,
As incense rises from the Homes of Prayer,
While the unfettered eyes, allured and rested,
Urge the forbidden lips to stoop and share;

Share in the sweetness of the rose and azure
Traced in the Dragon's form upon the white
Curve of the arm. Ah, curb thyself, my fancy,
Where would'st thou drift in this enchanted flight ?